the factory, as presently or[ganized]
the growth of free persona[l]

Sumner H. Slichter, in c[onsidering "The]
Position of Trade Unions i[n the American]
Economy," concludes t[hat "business]
unionism must seek to broaden its aims."

Although favoring new regulative legislation, Archibald Cox in "The Role of
Law in Preserving Union Democracy"
points out that "the law cannot create the
spirit of self-government."

In appraising "Union Self-Discipline
and the Freedom of Individual Workers,"
David L. Cole finds that "Labor itself can
do more to provide protection for individual workers, and can do it more quickly,
than can possibly be accomplished through
other means."

Expressing "A Trade Union Point of
View," Arthur J. Goldberg urges that, if
legislation affecting internal union affairs
is unavoidable, it should seek "to
strengthen, not to weaken, the system of
private law created by collective bargaining."

Hugh A. Clegg in "The Rights of British
Trade Union Members" and James R.
McClelland in "Experiences of the Australian Labor Movement under Governmental Control" describe the effects of
governmental supervision in two countries
where the labor movement has been
powerful for many years.

In a concluding chapter the editors summarize the discussions that followed the
presentation at the Arden House conference of each of these papers.

LABOR IN A FREE SOCIETY

EDITED BY MICHAEL HARRINGTON and PAUL JACOBS

LABOR IN A
FREE SOCIETY

WITH A FOREWORD BY **CLARK KERR**

UNIVERSITY OF CALIFORNIA PRESS

BERKELEY and LOS ANGELES / 1959

UNIVERSITY OF CALIFORNIA PRESS
BERKELEY AND LOS ANGELES, CALIFORNIA

CAMBRIDGE UNIVERSITY PRESS
LONDON, ENGLAND

*Seven contributions from the Arden House
Conference May, 1958, sponsored by the
Fund for the Republic, Inc.*

LIBRARY OF CONGRESS CATALOG CARD NUMBER: 59-11312

PRINTED IN THE UNITED STATES OF AMERICA

FOREWORD

It is a commonplace in our time to say that industrial society poses a basic challenge to those of us who are concerned with the extension of man's freedom. But too often this larger issue is discussed by itself without reference to the growing mass of data which we are accumulating. On the one side there are generalities, on the other, facts, and we regularly fail to define the relationship between the two.

The conference held in May, 1958, at Arden House, Harriman, N. Y., under the sponsorship of the Basic Issues Program of the Fund for the Republic, and attended by more than a hundred representatives from the labor movement, government, universities, management, and the field of arbitration, limited itself to "labor in a free society." And yet, the most striking thing about the three days of discussion from which the following papers are taken was the way in which debate over a very specific problem would suddenly reveal underlying and varied conceptions of man, freedom, and society. On the other hand, the more philosophic statements were constantly brought back to the immediate issues and examined on the basis of the rich, practical experience of the participants.

However, this volume does not attempt to present a comprehensive world view, or, for that matter, even answer all the specific questions raised. On the contrary, it is tentative, a contribution to a discussion which must go far beyond these

*and other beginnings. More than anything else, I hope it will
stimulate more thinking and more research, but always within
the context of defining and probing our basic values as they
relate to the actual situations which we face. In this, the
Trade Union Project of the Fund is itself but a part of a
larger task, that of exploring the new dimensions of freedom
—and of "unfreedom," to use Orwell's word—in this century
of technology.*

*Thus, I think that the conference, and this volume, perform
a very real function in terms of the Fund's over-all purpose—
to clarify fundamental questions concerning freedom and
justice that emerge when the forms and principles developed
by eighteenth-century America meet the ideas and practices
of today's highly developed industrial society. And one of our
fundamental problems is, as Henry Adams defined it a half
a century ago in his curious essay "The Rule of Phase Applied
to History" in* The Degradation of the Democratic Dogma:
*time is becoming faster, and like the transformation of ice to
water and then to steam, more volatile. In such a world, how
do we define fundamental values—and how do we make them
real?*

*The very quality of life in our society has been vastly trans-
formed since the Constitution was written. It is, of course, a
truism that we are no longer a nation of merchants and yeo-
men and pioneers; that we have become, perhaps more than
any other people, "modern." Yet, this thought is too often
simply related to issues of political structure. It is not given
its deeper meanings—meanings which pervade the very in-
terior of our lives.*

*The relevance of freedom to the self-sufficient farmer is
clear enough. Historically it has meant the right to till the
soil and mind one's own business. But how do we define freedom for the production worker? A few years ago, the United
Automobile Workers made a contract demand: that the man
on the line have the right to demote himself to the job of*

sweeper. In doing so, the union recognized the grinding, wearing effect on human beings who must pace themselves according to the rhythm of a machine. Yet, demotion is hardly a full answer! This problem was raised by Erich Fromm at the conference and his contribution to the discussion is included in this volume. His presentation provoked a vigorous discussion, for there were those who felt that our technology was progressively eliminating the monotonous and inhuman job. Again, no definitive conclusion was reached. Still, it is clear that we must confront this issue and that we must eventually reach conclusions about it, if we are really to measure up to the challenge of freedom in an industrial society.

Even here, in this most basic kind of discussion, we must take care not to omit new factors. The revolution of modern technology is a continuing one. Today, automation has gone into the business office, and if you pause to look at the administrative center of a large company, you will see white-collar workers whose duties are coming to resemble those of the production worker. There are long rows of business machines, and men and women who tend them, and in this it may be that office life is becoming factory-like. So even if we assume that those who disagreed with Fromm are right (and, for me, the issue is anything but settled), it is quite possible that our society is producing a new area of alienation.

And yet, I do not want to raise particular problems in this introduction. I simply want to emphasize once again that the development of our industrial society is changing the very way in which we live, that it is a factor in the most minute areas of our daily existence. Consequently, when we speak of defining a context for our discussion, we are dealing with a shifting context, a context in motion, and that makes our task all the more complex.

But then, if we become a little more specific, we can see how these elements of change affect the particular area with which this volume deals. Unions themselves are, of course, institutions which were unknown to the Constitutional Fathers. There is not a single sentence about them in the basic political documents of American democracy. Typically, we have developed our social policy toward this new labor movement empirically, on an ad hoc basis. This has the advantage of avoiding abstract, ideological counterpositions—but it involves the danger that we never get a real perspective on the problem before us. Instead, we face a series of isolated issues, of immediate crises. In some of these papers, there is an attempt to gain something of a vantage point, to see the larger movement which has emerged from our institutional inventions and compromises. This attempt goes to the very center of the Fund for the Republic's purpose.

Yet we are not in search of large and lifeless generalities. The AFL and the CIO have merged—the culmination of years of development within the American labor movement and American society as a whole. For many, one of the major virtues of this unity was that it put an end to fratricidal disputes between various unions, that it marked the establishment, in fact, of the "no-raiding" agreements. But now, if we did not anticipate the problem before, it is clear that an end to jurisdictional struggles has another side—that it closes off an avenue of protest which the locals, or the members, could utilize against an international administration. The threat to go to another union is no longer what it once was. Does this mean that we must compensate for this loss, that we must find more constructive channels for the kind of opposition that once expressed itself through local secession?

Or take another kind of question which developed in our discussion of these papers. One of the social gains of the past two decades has been the growth of various kinds of security for the worker. Through these plans, sickness, unemployment, and old age have been placed in a social context. But a correlative of this development has been a loss of mobility for the individual worker. Now he is much more tied to his place of work, to a single corporation, for if he leaves his job and moves on he suffers a considerable loss of accumulated rights. We would certainly not propose to meet this situation by reverting to the old conditions of insecurity. And yet, how shall we retain the positive freedom of movement while still eliminating the negative freedom to be insecure?

These are the kind of specifics which must be faced if we are to take seriously our task of redefining freedom in the modern environment—or better, our task of achieving freedom through understanding its relations to the modern environment. And yet, I have left an important element out of this brief survey. So far, I have presumed the assumption of shared values. But one of the characteristics of this dynamic world is that it produces a conflict of values even among men who start with the same good will and the same intelligence.

For example, what of the counterposition of values between centralization and local autonomy? How do these relate to freedom in our world? Traditionally, Americans have almost always answered the question with a policy of trying to maximize local autonomy. This is part of our history with its long record of suspicion toward distant authority. And yet, one of the papers in this volume suggests that an emphasis upon local autonomy may well be a way of limiting freedom in the society as a whole. David Cole analyzes the very controversial strike of the Motormen's Benevolent Association, a craft grouping which developed within the Transport Workers Union. To him, this action represented a dangerous assignment of priorities, placing the interests of a specific grouping on a higher plane than those of the union representing the majority of the workers, and above the interests of the people in the city who used the transportation system.

There were, of course, participants in the conference who disagreed sharply with Cole. That is not the point here. What is relevant is that it is quite possible to have differences on fairly basic values, in this case the relative worth of the local and autonomous unit as against centralized decision making, within the context of a common concern for freedom. The same kind of opposition appeared with regard to the purpose of trade unionism, another fundamental issue. There were those at the conference who felt that the unions must transcend their present mode of operation and become multifunctional if they were to respond adequately to the problem of freedom which they faced. And there were others who regarded this multifunctionalism as a threat to the individual's rights, as expressing a tendency toward the creation of an all-pervasive bureaucracy.

Thus, our task is not limited to defining our new situation and discovering techniques to cope with it. It also involves a debate over competing values and different predictions of how different courses of action will affect human freedom. In this, I think that the tentative character of this volume should have a salutary impact. For it reminds us once again that we are only at the beginning, that we face difficulties in every area of our endeavor. These difficulties, to return to the major theme of the Fund's work, are a consequence of the dynamic, moving society in which we live and for which we seek the values of a true democracy.

It is this perspective which I would suggest for a reading of these papers. In Fromm's contribution, there is an attempt to discuss the larger implications of the way in which industrialization and the growth of a consumer society affect our freedom. Sumner Slichter has provided a stimulating discussion of the changing role of the unions in the economy, and concludes with a proposal that the labor movement go beyond its present method of operation and develop a "new unionism." Archibald Cox presents an excellent summary of the different policy techniques that have been put forward in our current debate over labor legislation. Arthur Goldberg, writing from his varied personal experience as a labor lawyer, has produced a provocative treatment of the problem of com-

paring political democracy in our constitutional society to the structure of union internal life. And in the papers of Hugh Clegg and J. R. McClelland there is another perspective, that of comparing the position of labor in two nations with important union movements—England and Australia—two nations not too different from our own.

There is no formal continuity in this volume, no single narrative theme which links all of the papers together. But, at this stage of the discussion, that is as it should be. For the Fund for the Republic believes that the greatest contribution it can make is to present the work of informed and intelligent minds as they approach this crucial issue of freedom in the modern world from many angles. It is from this kind of work that an integrated view, even new conceptions of freedom, may perhaps eventually emerge.

CLARK KERR

Berkeley
January, 1959

CONTENTS

THE CONTRIBUTORS

ERICH FROMM is a psychoanalyst and author of numerous books.

SUMNER F. SLICHTER is Lamont Professor of Economics at Harvard University.

ARCHIBALD COX is Professor of Law at Harvard University and a former member of the National Wage Stabilization Board.

DAVID L. COLE is an arbitrator and former director of the Federal Mediation and Conciliation Service.

ARTHUR J. GOLDBERG is general counsel for the United Steelworkers of America and counsel for the AFL-CIO Ethical Practices Committee.

HUGH A. CLEGG is Bursar of Nuffield College, Oxford University, and author of numerous works on the British labor movement.

JAMES R. McCLELLAND is a labor attorney and counsel for the Federated Ironworkers Association of Australia.

MICHAEL HARRINGTON is a member of the editorial board of *Dissent,* a political journalist, and a participant in Fund for the Republic studies.

PAUL JACOBS is staff director of the Fund for the Republic Trade Union Project, a staff writer for *The Reporter,* and a former union representative.

ERICH FROMM

Freedom in the Work Situation

FREEDOM means many things to many people. Do we mean by freedom, a freedom *from*—freedom from drudgery, from monotony, from the stupidity of manual work, freedom from the irrational authority of a boss or foreman, freedom from exploitation? Or, on the other hand, do we mean a freedom *to*—freedom to participate actively in the work process or freedom to enjoy work? Actually our concept of freedom today is essentially a negative one:/It is freedom *from* and not freedom *to*, because we are mostly concerned with what we are *against* and not what we are *for*—against whom we should defend ourselves rather than what we are living for.

The word freedom shares this ambiguous quality with some other words that we frequently use. For instance, we use the word democracy and mean by it—more or less unconsciously—"consent manipulated without force." Or we use the word equality and mean by it sameness, rather than what equality meant originally: that no man must be the means toward the end of another man. Or we speak of happiness and really mean unrestricted consumption.

In discussing that ambiguous term, freedom, I will try to say something about the psychological problem of modern man in general, and the worker specifically.

Little needs to be said about the basic economic facts of twentieth-century capitalism as distinguished from the nine-

teenth century—just this much: today we live in an era of
mass production, both in the sense of production of great quan-
tity of commodities and in the sense of masses of people
working together in a well-organized, smooth way without
friction. Consumption is to some extent predictable by market
research; it is managed by advertising—by creating needs synthetically. Mass man is confronted with the four great bureaucracies: the bureaucracy of industry, of labor, of government,
and of the armed forces. These bureaucracies work together
and form a network which interacts with the mass man, who is
quite willing to be managed by them provided he has the illusion that his decisions are free and that he is "really" the one
who tells them what to do.

I should like to say a word about bureaucracy from a psychological standpoint because this has a bearing on what I
have to say later. Bureaucracy is not simply administration. In
any differentiated society we need administration of things,
and we need even a certain amount of regulation of people.
What I mean by bureaucracy is the administration of men *as
if they were things;* or, to quote Marx, to relate to men as objects. This attitude is inherent in every bureaucracy. The problem of bureaucracy, in the sense I have in mind, is not the
question of cruel versus human treatment of people. When we
think of the Russians, we always emphasize that they treat
the people cruelly. This is not the point here. Furthermore,
the problem is not only one of bureaucracy—as if bureaucracy
took over and the unwilling people were forced to submit to
it. Bureaucracy is a relationship between the bureaucrat and
his objects, the people. The bureaucrat treats people as things,
and people agree to be treated as things as long as they don't
know it, as long as they have their initials on their sportshirts
or handbags, as long as they have the illusion of individuality
and freedom.

Modern capitalism, then, needs men who coöperate smoothly
and in large numbers, who want to consume ever more, and

whose tastes are standardized and can be easily influenced and anticipated; men who feel free and independent—not subject to any authority or principle or conscience—yet willing to be commanded to do what is expected of them, to fit into the social machine without friction; to be guided without force, led without leader, prompted without aim—except the one to make good—to be on the move, to function, to go ahead.

The paradox in the relationship between the bureaucrats and their followers is that the bureaucrats have no aim and the followers have no aim, but each group thinks that the other one has an aim. That is to say, the followers think the bureaucrats know what they are doing and where they are going; and the bureaucrats, in a vague sense, think that their followers have told them where to go. Actually the two are like the two blind men who walk on the street each thinking the other sees.

We are concerned with instrumentalities—with *how* we are doing things; we are no longer concerned with *why* we are doing things. We build machines that act like men and we want to produce men who act like machines. Our danger today is not that of becoming slaves, but of becoming automatons.

Indeed, means have become ends. Material production once was supposed to be a means for a more dignified, happier life, and the aim was clearly the fuller, more dignified, more human life. Today production and consumption have become ends in themselves. Nobody asks any longer, why or what for? We are happy discovering how we can produce more. In fact, our economic system is based on ever-increasing consumption and production. But why we want to produce more, why we want this, that, and the other—this is a question which is not asked.

Let us take another example. We are all eager to save time. But what do we do with the time we have saved? We are embarrassed and we try to kill it. Anyone who knows the present-day situation realizes what would happen to the United States

if we had a general 20-hour work week today. We would have
thousands more psychiatrists to take care of the nervous break-
downs which would occur if people had that much more free
time on their hands without knowing what to do with it.

Our consumption also is an end in itself. You might say that
modern man's concept of heaven is a tremendous department
store with new things every day, and with enough money to
buy everything he pleases. We are the eternal sucklings, drink-
ing in cigarettes and lectures and movies and television. Many
people speak of love as one talks of milk. "The child didn't get
enough love, it didn't get enough affection." You drink it in.
That is exactly the picture described in the *Brave New World*
by Huxley. "Why postpone a satisfaction until tomorrow when
you can have it today?"

If I may add a footnote: It has been said that the change in
sex mores which happened after 1914 is due to Freud. I think
this is erroneous. Freud above all was a Puritan and nothing
was further from his thoughts then the advocacy of uninhib-
ited sexual activity. Freud was only used for the purposes of
our consumption craziness. We want to satisfy every need
immediately—the need for sex, a car, television.

To speak from another standpoint, man, being preoccupied
with the production of things, has unconsciously transformed
himself into a thing. Consciously we talk about our dignity
and all the things which are based on a tradition of hundreds
and even thousands of years. But actually, most people unconsciously speak of themselves as things and treat each other as
things. A person might come to a psychoanalyst—a person he
has never seen before—and tell his tragic life story as if he
complained to a garage mechanic that the car has stalled. This
problem is related to a central issue—to the phenomenon of
alienation. The term comes from Hegel; it was a central issue
with Marx; and all existentialist philosophy is a reaction to
alienation—from Kierkegaard to Sartre and in the most significant existentialist philosopher, Marx.

It is one of the peculiar phenomena of our present-day culture that, aside from the Old Testament, there is hardly any book which is so much talked about as Marx and so little known. The Russians have claimed that they represent Marx's ideas, yet they represent exactly the opposite. They are the most reactionary regime in Europe. I am not speaking of the terror but of their school system, their social relations; they are about where Europe was in 1830, in a period of fast accumulation of capital. But certainly they have nothing whatever to do with the aims of Marx, and we do them a tremendous service by confirming to the world their own claim that they represent the aims of Marx.

To talk about alienation we might start with a concept which is clear to anyone who knows the Old Testament—the concept of *idolatry*. The prophets had as their main object the fight against idolatry. This is often understood to mean that they believed in one god and the others in many gods and that this numerical difference is the point of monotheism. But this is not so at all. The concept of idolatry is clearly defined in the Old Testament as man bowing down and worshiping the work of his own hands. As one of the prophets expressed it so beautifully: Here you have a piece of wood; one half you take and make a fire and warm yourself, or boil your meat; with the other half you make a statue, and this statue you worship as your god. Or as one of the psalms said: "They have ears and they do not hear; they have eyes and they do not see; they have hands and they do not touch." That is to say, man disowns his own creative power, transfers it to an object and then worships his own power in an alienated form, by worshiping the idol. He does not experience himself any more as a creator, as a subject of these powers; he is in touch with himself only by the indirect and alienated way of being in touch with that which his own power has created. A quotation from Marx shows how closely related his definition is to the concept of idolatry in the Old Testament. Marx said, "Man's

own act becomes to him an alien power, standing over and
against him instead of being ruled by him." And he goes on to
say that all history is also the history of man's alienation from
himself and from his own human power; that history is the
consolidation of our own product to an objective power above
us—outgrowing our control, defeating our expectations, alien-
ating our calculations; that man has been the object of circumstances; and that he must become the subject so that man becomes the highest theme for man.

The history of the Christian Church provides another example of idolatry. What was Luther protesting against when he
separated from the Catholic Church? There were many issues,
but one of them was that in the Church man faced God only
through the bureaucracy of the Church, through the priests.
In other words, man was alienated from God; he did not face
God directly but was instead in touch with a priest through
whom he was put in touch with God. So Luther protests, insist-
ing that each man is an individual who should and can be in
direct touch with God.

This Lutheran tradition is one of the bases of our modern
concept of freedom and individuality. And yet what do we see
today? We see exactly the same situation that Luther fought.
Church membership and participation in services is, relatively,
the highest in a hundred years. And what is the result? Ours is
a very unreligious culture. Here we see the fact of alienation.
By belonging to a church, by attending a service on Sunday,
the individual has the conscious feeling of being in touch with
God—with his own spiritual powers. But in reality it is idolatry
and alienation because he does not have a religious experience.
He only has a quasi-religious experience by being in touch
with those powers to whom the religious experience is rele-
gated.

The same happens in our social situation. The American
citizen today is concerned almost exclusively with private
problems. By "concerned," I mean enough interested in a

problem to lose one's sleep sometimes, not merely just to talk about it. He loses his sleep about health, money, and family problems. He does not lose his sleep about problems of society, because he has cut himself off from the experiences of social concern, from the relatedness to others as part of his life. He is a private individual with only private interests, separated from a general interest in the whole, and has projected his social relatedness to government, to the specialist. If he goes to the polls, which 40 per cent to 50 per cent never do, then he does about the same as going to church on Sunday. He is under the illusion that by being in touch with those who represent him as a social being, he himself experiences his social relatedness. He does not.

We as a nation are being ruled by things and circumstances, and there was never an age in which the fact was demonstrated in such a terrifying way as today. Because today, indeed, we are ruled by the bomb. The bomb is something of our making. The circumstances, the various governments are things of our making; and yet we have become almost helpless prisoners of circumstances which might lead any day to the destruction of everything alive and everything we value. We know this fact, yet we do not experience the effect of fear, horror, and protest that a normal person would experience. This split between thought and affect, a mechanism characteristic for schizophrenia, is characteristic for modern man. Yet, because we *all* suffer from it, we do not consider it pathological.

The result of this alienated schizoid life is something for which the French had a word one hundred and fifty years ago. They called it *la malaise du siècle*—the illness of the century, or ennui. Today we call it neurotic. We are indoctrinated not to feel unhappy, because if you feel unhappy you are not a success. But you are permitted to feel neurotic. So you go to the doctor, and you say you suffer from insomnia or you "have a problem." You have a car, you have a wife, you have kids, you have a house—you have a problem. Our way of thinking and feeling is that all the emphasis is not on "to be" but on "to have." We *have* much—but we *are* little. This attitude leads to defeatism, although it may be unconscious.

I believe, for instance, that although we all pretend to believe in democracy, many people believe in democracy only in the sense, as I said before, of "consent manipulated without force," and not in democracy as the voluntary, active, productive participation of responsible citizens. We all repeat formulas in which we have, at best, a half-hearted belief. As a result of this, we are insecure, we lack the sense of identity based on our convictions and our faith, and we get a sense of identity only by conformity; that is, I know that I am I—not because I have a conviction, not because I feel intensity, but because I am like everybody else. And if I am three feet away from the herd, that makes me very insecure because then I don't know any more who I am.

I would like to discuss now specifically the problem of work and the worker in the United States. This is difficult, because the working class in this country is not a sharply limited class today as it was in Europe and in the United States a hundred years ago. In many ways, psychologically speaking, the working class today belongs to the middle class just as everybody else psychologically belongs or tries to belong to the middle class.

What are some of the differences between the situation of the worker in the nineteenth and twentieth centuries? The worker in the nineteenth century was exploited and excluded from humanity. The average nineteenth-century capitalist had no feeling of identity with the worker, just as he had none with people of other races. Actually he could exploit the worker to the extent that he did only if he did not identify himself with the worker; and the capitalist had to exploit the worker for the purpose of the accumulation of capital.

The worker in the nineteenth century did not work as the

middle class did, on the basis of a Protestant-Puritan "drive for work"; he did not like his work—he worked because he had to. Work was essentially forced labor, and work was stupid. As a reaction to this inhuman situation of the worker, there arose the movement which was, in my opinion, one of the few genuinely religious movements in the nineteenth century, although it was not perceived in such terms. With the introduction of labor unions the worker began to experience his own sense of human dignity and solidarity, his sense of self, his own human powers. He had a vision of a nonalienated, humanistic society. The movement of labor unions had as its aim, of course, higher wages and a better standard of living— but by no means was this the only goal, and maybe not even the main one. This movement, like socialism, was originally a humanistic, a spiritual movement of human liberation and solidarity.

The situation of the worker today is different. The worker today is also the consumer—and I mean the consumer in the psychological sense. Of course, he was always a consumer because he had to eat and drink. But he is now a consumer with the same craving for consuming that the members of all other classes have. The worker is not only part of the great consumers' mass whose tastes and desires are manipulated by industry; he is also manipulated by the industrial bureaucracy in his work situation, by the union bureaucracy through his membership in the union, by the government bureaucracy because he is a citizen, and, if he gets drafted or otherwise comes in contact with the armed forces, he is manipulated by that bureaucracy too.

The worker has the same private and alienated concern for himself. The worker today does not dream so much of becoming president of General Motors or anything of that sort. But the new car, the new house, the new television set, the larger refrigerator—these are his dreams. These are his convictions, these are his hopes. He is caught in the net of bureaucracies; he is the alienated mass man, headed in the same direction of human automation as the whole society.

What is the meaning of work today? The generally accepted aim of our social effort is held to be increase of production and consumption. There is an axiom: What is good for production is good for the worker. And in the past few years the belief has gained ground that what is good for the worker is good for production. This new axiom has furthered efforts in the study of what is called "human relations," "industrial psychology," "human engineering," and all that kind of thing. One discovers that if the worker is happier he produces more effectively, and, since the aim is to produce more effectively, the conclusion is by all means—let him be happy. Then the question arises—what can we do to make him happy? The assumption is, axiomatically, that all the things which correspond to our ideology—participation, democracy in the work situation—make also for greater efficiency and productivity of work. There are many studies which prove this, but there are some studies which prove that sometimes it is not so—for instance, that a greater participation in work may not make for greater productivity.

Here we come to a basic problem of value. It is all very nice if the happy, democratic, participating worker also produces more. Such preordained harmony between the aims of production and the aims of man is wonderful. But what if it is not so? Are we in favor of participation in work as a democratic process even though it might lead to somewhat less production? This question is simply not raised, and most of our psychologists try to ignore it. We have the same problem today with regard to political democracy. You find many people who say democracy of course is very good. But what should happen if we find out that we are less efficient than the Russians? Should we still use our democratic system? Or should we say it is just a myth and we have to have a managed society instead of one based on the active, responsible participation of each citizen? We talk all the time about our ideas, our principles, and yet in reality we shy away from making value judgments which will commit us. Those judgments can be made only if one confronts the possibility that one may not combine the best of both worlds—God's and Caesar's—and there the problem begins. As long as one assumes that there cannot be a conflict between democratic procedure and maximum efficiency, one does not truly judge.

I am reminded of the title of Elton Mayo's famous book, *The Human Problem of an Industrial Society.* The title tells the whole story (although Mayo had his heart on the side of man). Industry is a subject and it *has* a human problem. The question is whether we talk about the human problem of industry or whether we talk about the industrial problem of humanity. In the latter case, humanity is the subject which has an industrial problem. Between these two formulations lies the difference between two opposite philosophical, spiritual value judgments.

We come now to the crucial question: What are the conditions to make the worker happy? There are two main answers. One is that the worker can be happy within the work situation. Many suggestions are made to achieve this aim, such as profit-sharing—an appeal to the worker's interest in increased profit and often a concealed antiunion attitude; or making the worker feel that he participates—but the *feeling* that one participates is not necessarily the same as the *fact* of participating. Much of what is recommended as participation is fiction. The most important field in which one tries to make the worker happier today is called human relations, largely promoted by psychologists. Here a strange process is going on: In the name of the ideas of Spinoza and Freud, and particularly in the name of Socrates' idea that man should know himself in order to be himself, the very opposite is done. Man is manipulated and smoothed out to such an extent that nothing of his individuality is left. These so-called human relations are to a large extent based on an alienated concept of life: that man is a thing and that there's a specialist to deal with this thing. If you belong to the middle or upper class you talk with a Freudian on a couch and with a non-Freudian in a comfortable chair, and you might have the idea that if you have talked long enough you will end up as the well-rounded happy person who has no problems. But if you are a worker, this is not possible. It is much too expensive to talk for years, for one thing. Instead, the talking is done for a few hours. That is in itself very nice in a culture in which nobody listens anyway. We are all polite to each other, like each other quite generally, and are not hostile. That is one of the good traits of our present-day American society. But we are essentially indifferent to each other and we do not want to listen. Hence one can speak to somebody who is paid to listen for one or two or five hours and perhaps sometimes even listens with interest—that is in itself a pleasant or quieting experience. It helps to bear the drudgery of life for another year and then one may go back to the man and talk again. I do not mean to imply that all industrial psychology is of this alienated type. But I do want to point to the danger that psychology is often used for the purpose of further alienation and manipulation and that human relations in industry become the most inhuman relations one could imagine—inhuman not in the sense of cruelty but in the sense of alienation, of the "re-ification" of man—the treatment of man as a thing.

The other answer to the problem of the worker's happiness is exactly the opposite. Since the worker can never be happy in work, this answer says, there is only one solution: as little work as possible, as mechanized work as possible and he will be happy in his free time. This answer is accepted by many people, and in many ways it is a very plausible answer, considering the fact that the working week has changed from more than 70 hours in 1850 to 40 hours in 1950, that we are coming closer to a 35-hour week, and that it is not at all fantastic to think of a 20-hour week in the future. All this, from the standpoint of the nineteenth century, would have seemed the most alluring Utopia.

But I cannot see that leisure as the answer to the worker's happiness is satisfactory. Leisure today means essentially consumption and passivity. A man who works 20 hours a week would turn into the complete consumer; he would be exactly like the man in Huxley's *Brave New World;* he would lack the inner creativity or productivity which is the condition of genuine happiness. Work is not only an economical problem but a profoundly human problem.

My own ideas about the satisfaction and happiness of the worker are presented in my book *The Sane Society.* I have attempted to show there that the goal for the worker as well as for all other members of society must be to overcome the alienation and re-ification which pervades society. *Man must cease to be the consumer and become a productive human being* who is aware of and responds to his world creatively. This means, applied to the worker, that he must become a responsible and active participant in the whole process of work. There are many possibilities for more active interest and participation in the work process itself. (Georges Friedmann in his works has given important suggestions in this direction.) Increased technical knowledge could make even routine work more interesting. Furthermore, the factory is more than a combination of machines—it is an economic and social entity. Even if the work itself is boring, each worker can participate actively in the economic planning and the considerations preceding it, and in the organization and administration of the factory as a social unit where man spends the larger part of his life.

All this requires active participation of the worker in the management of the factory. How this can be achieved legally and socially is a question which transcends this discussion. Ways and means can be found, provided one recognizes the importance of the aim. One specific point, however, I wish to make. I wish to emphasize the error of popular Socialist thinking—misunderstanding the essential idea of socialism —that the most important point is the change from private to public ownership of the means of production. This idea was based on the overestimation of legal ownership characteristic for the nineteenth century. Today we can differentiate between legal ownership of a big enterprise (the stockholders) and social ownership (the management, which controls the enterprise without legally owning it). The problem of the future is to restore to man his initiative and activity. Applied to the worker, that means that work in the factory, technically, economically, and socially, becomes meaningful to him because he becomes an active participant in managing the life of the factory. Only then can he make use also of his leisure time in a productive way rather than as a passive consumer.

The worker can be the leader in the movement to overcome alienation and to bring the reintegration of man, because, in some ways, he is less caught than those who deal with symbols —figures or men. The manual worker sells his energy and his skill but not his "personality." This makes a great difference. His efficiency, his work, do not depend on whether he is a nice "personality package." The respect of his co-workers does not depend on that. It depends on how reliable he is; how well he performs his functions. In some ways, therefore, I would say there are possibilities for the worker to be less alienated than for the average person. I would say there is another possibility, the union movement, provided it could, instead of being a bureaucracy manipulating alienated men, become again a movement in which general and unalienated solidarity is expressed among men who share the same basic experience—their work. That, of course, would require the workers and the union leaders to have a different picture of what the function of a union should be. But I believe the union could perform an important function in helping to change our history from the dangerous course of ever-increasing alienation to a direction in which man counts again, and in which he is not the *object* of circumstances that he has created but their *master.*

I believe it is necessary to realize that changes must be made in all spheres of culture simultaneously. It was a mistake of religion to think that one can make a change in the spiritual sphere alone and leave out the other sections of life. It was a mistake when those who misunderstood Marx proclaimed in his name that one can make a change in the economic sphere alone and everything good will follow. It was a mistake of political democracy to think that one can make a change in the political sphere alone. Effective changes can be made only if they are made in all spheres together, because man is not compartmentalized. One step in an integrated way is more important than twenty steps in one sphere to the exclusion of the others.

Our only alternative to the danger of robotism is humanistic communitarianism. The problem is not primarily the legal problem of property ownership, nor that of sharing profits; it is that of sharing work, sharing experience. Changes in ownership must be made to the extent necessary to create a community of work, and to prevent the profit motive from directing production into socially harmful directions. Income must be equalized to the extent of giving everybody the material basis for a dignified life and thus preventing economic differences from creating a fundamentally different experience of life among various social classes. Man must be reinstituted in his supreme place in society—never a means, never a thing to be used by others or by himself. Man's use by man must end, and economy must become the servant for the development of man. Capital must serve labor; things must serve life. Instead of the exploitative and hoarding orientation dominant in the nineteenth century, and the receptive and marketing orientation dominant today, the *productive orientation* must be the end that all social arrangements serve. Freedom in the work situation is not freedom *from* work (in order to have leisure), it is not freedom from crude exploitation; it is the freedom *to* spend one's energy in a meaningful, productive way by being an active, responsible, unalienated participant in the total work situation. The unions, by starting to introduce such participation within their own organization can make a first step in the direction of freedom at the work bench.

SUMNER H. SLICHTER

The Position of Trade Unions in the American Economy

THE two most important facts about the state of industrial relations in the United States today are (1) the general and searching examination of unions, their internal operations, their relations with each other, their impact on the community, and their place in the economy, that began more than ten years ago and that has been going on ever since, and (2) the substantial progress that is being made in the development of stable and, on the whole, mutually satisfactory relations between unions and employers in most enterprises where unions are established.

The examination of trade unions that is being made is broad and persistent. It relates to the objectives of trade unions, their internal operations, their policies, their activities, and the activities of their officers. It began more than ten years ago when the Taft-Hartley Act was passed. It is being carried out by many parts of the community—by committees of Congress and of state legislatures, by scholars, and by unions themselves and their leaders.[1] The strong interest in trade

---

[1] Papers and studies by scholars include my paper entitled *Trade Unions in a Free Society*, Harvard University Press, 1948; Philip Taft, "The Constitutional Power of the Chief Officer in American Trade Unions," *Quarterly Journal of Economics* (May, 1948), "Status of Members in Unions During Appeal from a Penalty," *ibid.* (August, 1948),

unions is a result of the great upsurge in union membership in the past twenty-five years. Activities and policies of unions that did not matter when union membership was small, are matters of public concern today. Trade unions have lost the comfortable privilege of being ignored—a privilege reserved for the weak. They must endure the scrutiny and the criticism that are reserved for the strong.

At the same time that various parts of the community are taking a searching look at union activities, trade unions and employers are making important progress in adapting themselves to each other and in working out stable and satisfactory relationships. Progress between unions and employers has apparently been little affected by the general examination of unions and their activities that has been going on and by some of the resulting changes in public policy, such as the substitution of the Taft-Hartley Act for the Wagner Act.

This paper falls into five parts. First, I shall examine some of the principal effects on the trade-union movement that re-

and "Corruption and Racketeering in the Labor Movement," *Bulletin*, Ithaca, N.Y.: New York School of Industrial and Labor Relations, Cornell University (February, 1958); Clyde Summers, "Disciplinary Powers of Unions," *Industrial and Labor Relations Review* (July, 1950) and "Disciplinary Procedures of Unions," *ibid.* (October, 1950); John Dunlop, "Structural Changes in the American Labor Movement and Industrial Relations System," *Proceedings* of the Ninth Annual Meeting of the Industrial Relations Research Association, Cleveland, Ohio, 1956, and "The Public Interest in the Internal Affairs of Unions," mimeographed; George W. Brooks, "Reflections on the Changing Character of American Labor Unions," *Proceedings* of the Ninth Annual Meeting of the Industrial Relations Research Association, Cleveland, Ohio, 1956; Archibald Cox, "The Taft-Hartley Act After Six Years," *Proceedings* of the Fifth Annual Conference on Industrial Relations, Buffalo, N.Y., 1953; E. E. Witte's paper "The Crisis in American Unionism," given before the National Academy of Arbitrators in St. Louis, Montana, January 31, 1958; Clark Kerr, *Unions and Union Leaders of Their Own Choosing*, New York: Fund for the Republic, 1957; Roscoe Pound, "Legal Immunities of Trade Unions" and E. H. Chamberlin, "Economic Analysis of Labor Union Power" in E. H. Chamberlin and others, *Labor Unions and Public Policy*, Washington, D.C.: American Enterprise Association, 1955; and Malcolm Johnson, *Crime on the Labor Front*, New York: McGraw-Hill, 1950.

sulted from the decision of the country to encourage collective bargaining and trade unions; second, I shall explore a few problems that have been created for unions and the community; third, I shall summarize briefly some of the principal steps that have been taken in dealing with these problems; fourth, I shall discuss briefly the progress that has been made by trade unions and employers in working out mutually satisfactory relationships; and finally, I shall comment on the present general position of trade unions in the community.

II

The principal reason for the great upsurge in union membership in the past twenty-five years has been the change in public policy that occurred in 1933—though the depression of the 'thirties, the war, and the postwar boom were important reënforcing influences. The great depression led the country to believe that employees needed greater bargaining power relative to employers. The country observed what limited progress unions had made in the face of stern opposition from employers—even at the peak of prosperity in 1929, less than 11 per cent of the nonsupervisory, nonprofessional employees outside of agriculture had been organized.[2] Consequently, the country, in the face of stubborn opposition from business interests, adopted the policy of encouraging collective bargaining—first by the National Industrial Recovery Act in 1933 and later by the Wagner Act.

The Wagner Act did not require that labor contracts be negotiated by collective bargaining, but it did impose on the employer the obligation to bargain if the employees desired collective bargaining, and the government provided machinery

---

[2] In 1929, when trade-union membership was about 3,400,000, the total labor force was 48,600,000, of whom 2,900,000 were professional workers, 9,700,000, proprietors and managers, and 4,200,000 farm, laborers.

to settle representation disputes. Few governments regulate industrial relations more minutely than the government of the United States—though the original intention was simply to encourage collective bargaining.

The public policy of encouraging collective bargaining meant more than the passage of a couple of statutes—it led to a constitutional revolution. The National Industrial Recovery Act was thrown out for reasons not related to its bearing on collective bargaining, but the upholding of the Wagner Act, accomplished only by a 5 to 4 vote of the Supreme Court, required that the court adopt new conceptions of the scope of the commerce clause and that it reverse well-established interpretations of the Fifth Amendment.

III

Helped by public policy and later by the war and the postwar boom, trade-union membership in the United States shot up from 2,900,000 at the bottom of the depression in 1932 to 9,000,000 in 1939, 14,800,000 in 1945, and 17,800,000 in 1956.[3] In other words, more than five-sixths of the present trade-union membership has been acquired since the change in public policy in 1933. Trade-union members comprise about 34 per cent of the 51,500,000 nonprofessional and nonsupervisory employees. But the great upsurge in trade-union membership did not extend equally to all parts of the nonprofessional and nonsupervisory employees. The great majority of trade unionists, about 15,000,000, are concentrated among the 31,000,000 craftsmen, operatives, service workers, and non-

---

[3] Leo Wolman, *Ebb and Flow in Trade Unionism* (New York: National Bureau of Economic Research, 1936); U.S. Bureau of the Census, *Statistical Abstract of the United States, 1957*, Washington, D.C.: 1957, p. 232; Industrial Conference Board, *Management Record* (December, 1957), p. 414; *Monthly Labor Review* (October, 1957), pp. 1202–1210. Excluded from these figures are about 1,000,000 members of American trade unions in Canada. There are included about 500,000 workers in 300 single-firm independent unions.

agricultural workers. Only about 2,500,000 trade unionists are found among the 13,600,000 clerical and sales workers.[4] Among the 6,000,000 private-household workers and farm laborers, there are virtually no union members.

The concentration of trade-union membership among craftsmen, operatives, service workers, and nonagricultural laborers sheds light on the economic strength and on the political weakness of trade unions. The high proportion of craftsmen, operatives, and service workers who are union members helps the unions to influence wages and working conditions among those employees. On the other hand, the slim membership of unions among white collar and agricultural employees limits the opportunity of unions to influence the ideas of these workers.

There is little mixing of white-collar workers and blue-collar workers in the same unions. Ninety-five out of 184 unions report no white-collar members at all and 33 more report that less than 10 per cent of their members are white-collar workers. On the other hand, nearly two-thirds of the white-collar membership of unions is concentrated in 42 unions in which 70 per cent or more of the members are white-collar workers. Only 14 unions report a white-collar membership of more than 10 per cent, but less than 70 per cent.[5]

The failure of the great upsurge in union membership of the past twenty-five years to produce much effect among the clerical and sales workers, the private-household workers, and the farm laborers is important because it suggests (though it does not prove) that a large part of these employees do not care for unionism and will not be easy to organize. The reasons why the clerical and sales workers, private-household workers, and farm laborers did not organize when every-

[4] *Monthly Labor Review* (October, 1957), p. 1207. This is a rough estimate of the number of so-called white collar members in unions. Included in the 2,500,000 are a small number of technical and professional workers.

[5] *Monthly Labor Review* (October, 1957), p. 1207.

one else was doing so are various. As for the clerical and sales workers, who might have been expected to join the movement to organize, 64 per cent of the clerical workers and 38 per cent of the sales workers are women. But trade unions are in the main men's organizations run by and for men. More than four-fifths of trade-union members are male, and among the craftsmen, operatives, service workers, and nonfarm laborers, where trade-union membership is concentrated, about four-fifths of the jobs are held by men. Even the several unions composed in the main of women are led by male officers.

The government's encouragement of collective bargaining has apparently not affected the degree of concentration of membership in large unions. In 1956 the ten largest unions had about 45 per cent of the members.[6] In 1929, the proportion was 44.5 per cent, in 1920, 43.6 per cent, and back in 1900, 52.3 per cent.[7] But the government's encouragement of collective bargaining has probably helped small unions to survive. When they win representation rights, they acquire status that helps them withstand raids from other unions, and they are protected by law against some kinds of unfair labor practices by other unions. Unfortunately, there are no figures showing how small unions do in election contests with large unions, but most unions not affiliated with the AFL-CIO are small, and there are figures showing that unaffiliated unions hold their own in representation election contests with affiliated unions.[8] In 1956–57 the unaffiliated unions won slightly more than half of the elections in which they were pitted

---

[6] U.S. Bureau of Labor Statistics, *Directory of National and International Labor Unions in the United States, 1957, Bulletin No. 1222*, Washington, D.C.: 1957, p. 11.

[7] Leo Wolman, *op. cit.*, pp. 16, 172–193.

[8] In 1956, only 12 out of 52 national unions unaffiliated with the AFL-CIO had a membership of 25,000 or more, and 33 out of the 52 had a membership of less than 10,000. The average membership of unaffiliated national unions in 1956 was 30,200; of affiliated national unions, 122,000.

against affiliated unions—124 elections out of 245.[9] The number of small national unions (with 25,000 or fewer members) has shown little change in recent years. It was 94 in 1949 and in 1951, then it rose to 101 in 1954, dropped to 100 in 1955, and to 89 in 1956.[10] In addition to the small national unions, there are, as I have pointed out, at least 300 single-plant or single-company unions with about 500,000 members.

IV

When the people of the United States decided to encourage collective bargaining and trade unions by public policy, the trade-union movement here, though limited in size, was not new. Forty-one of the national unions in existence in 1933 had been formed before 1890, 72 before 1900, and the American Federation of Labor had been in existence 47 years. This trade-union movement had proud traditions, a well-developed philosophy, and well-established policies and methods.

The decision of the country to encourage collective bargaining did more than make it easier for trade unions to gain new members; it produced far-reaching and unintended effects. It forced the trade-union movement to abandon the principle of exclusive jurisdiction on which the AFL was founded and substantially to modify its other basic principle—the principle of the autonomy of the affiliated national unions. Some of the present problems of unions either stem

[9] A few years earlier, in 1950, the unaffiliated unions did not do so well —they won 347 representation elections out of 753 in which they competed with AFL affiliates, CIO affiliates, or both.

[10] An unspecified part of the drop from 100 to 89 was the failure of some unions in 1956 to meet the U.S. Bureau's interstate standard for inclusion. The rest of the drop was attributable to mergers or termination of activities. U.S. Bureau of Labor Statistics, *Directory of Labor Unions in the United States, 1950*, pp. 17–51; *ibid., 1953*, pp. 14–31; and *Directory of National and International Labor Unions in the United States, 1955*, pp. 25–43; *Monthly Labor Review* (October, 1957), p. 1206.

from the unintended effects of the government's policy or have
been aggravated by those effects.

On the other hand, some of the most important characteristics of American trade unions have not been significantly
changed by the government's policy. For example, the concentration of American unions on the employee-employer bargain has not changed—in fact, it has been increased. Even
the great increase in trade-union membership has not led
unions to put much steam behind such an obvious political
program as improving substantially the inadequate benefits
of the old-age-pension plan or the unemployment-compensa-
tion plan. On the contrary, the obligation imposed by law on
employers to bargain over pensions and other insurance items
has encouraged unions to bargain over these matters and has
weakened their interest in legislation. Likewise unchanged
has been the strong traditional interest of American unions
in shop practices and in rules and policies pertaining to ap-
prenticeship, work scheduling, layoffs, transfers, promotions,
technological changes, overtime, setting of piece rates and
production standards, and administration of discipline. Indeed, it has been difficult for American trade unionists to
understand the weak influence of European unions in the
shops. The obligation to bargain, imposed by law on employers, has accentuated the interest of American unions in shop
conditions.

v

But the changes introduced into the trade-union movement by
the policy of encouraging collective bargaining have been
numerous and important. One of the first effects was a great
temporary increase in grass-roots organizing—the springing
up of local unions by the hundreds in various plants in the
electrical industry, automobile industry, rubber industry, meat
packing industry, and many others. These were industrial

unions. Some of them acquired federal charters from the AFL, but many remained independent and helped organize national industrial unions that later challenged the jurisdiction of existing unions. Some of the grass-roots unions are still independent. But, as I have pointed out, the grass-roots organizing movement spread very little to the white-collar workers.

A second development was a fierce controversy among established unions over how to take advantage of the organizing opportunities created by the new public policy—a controversy which split the trade-union movement. Ten unions left the AFL under the leadership of Mr. Lewis to form first the Committee for Industrial Organization and later a rival federation, the Congress of Industrial Organizations.

A third result was a great increase in rivalry among unions for members. The trade-union movement in the United States had been built on the idea that the exclusive right to organize given categories of workers should belong to the union whose jurisdiction was recognized and approved by the AFL—the principle of exclusive jurisdiction. The excellent organizing opportunities created by the new public policy caused nearly all unions to ignore traditional jurisdictional lines. Furthermore, new national unions were formed—between 1933 and 1949 the number of national unions increased from 140 to 204.[11] Many of the new unions were rivals of existing unions.

A fourth result of government encouragement of collective bargaining was a broadening of the area and the scope of agreements between unions and employers. Unions have shown little tendency to attempt to negotiate on an industry-wide basis, but there has been a considerable growth of agreements covering a large part of a state (and for the teamsters, a number of states) and a considerable number of company-

---

[11] U.S. Bureau of Labor Statistics, *Directory of Labor Unions in the United States, 1950*, p. 4.

wide, or at least multiplant agreements. The scope of agreements has been extended to new subjects. This is particularly
true of the agreements of industrial unions which had had
to concern themselves with plant wage structures, production
standards, and problems of job classification. Agreements
providing for pension and health-and-welfare plans have been
due to several conditions, including the wage stabilization
policies of the war years, but their growth was encouraged
by the obligation of employers to bargain on these matters
and by the growing size and strength of unions. Broadening
the area and scope of trade agreements is important because it
increases the participation of the national officers of unions in
negotiations.

But by far the most important result of the policy of encouraging collective bargaining has been the general rise in
the importance of unions and the consequent growing public
interest in what unions do, what policies they pursue, and
how they conduct their affairs. For example, when unions
were small and of limited scope, the public tolerated the
closed shop and the control over employment opportunities
that it represented. But when unions controlled all or
nearly all the jobs in many important industries, the closed
shop was outlawed in interstate commerce, and the union
shop was substituted for it. The public was unwilling to give
private organizations such control over men's opportunities
to make a living, as is conferred by the closed shop.

The growing size and prosperity of trade unions and the
increasing number of company-wide agreements have affected
trade-union government. The nature of the work of administering the contracts, especially in manufacturing industries,
has developed many union representatives who have a good
grasp of shop-operating problems. Some of these men have
been lost to unions by becoming foremen, but many have remained with the locals and some have been placed on the
national staffs. The growth of unions has brought to the top

a number of able new union presidents and vice-presidents. For the most part, the new generation of leaders are better administrators than the earlier officers. Unions are making increased use of staff work.

The changes in trade-union government tend to shift power and control from the members of the unions to the leaders—though this is not a new trend.[12] Whether one regards this shift as desirable or undesirable depends upon a personal value judgment. For my part, I regard the shift, in the main, as desirable because it relieves union members of the necessity of participating in the decisions on many questions on which they are ill-informed; but it leaves them the opportunity to participate in making the most vital decisions, such as the selection of officers or delegates to conventions, determination of strike action, and, in some cases, the ratification of agreements.

As long as union membership was small, the effect of unions upon money wages was not of general concern. The effect of unions on the geographical structure of wages in some industries (steel, automobiles, rubber, and cans, for example) has been fairly pronounced, but does not seem to have created major problems. But the interoccupational wage structure that has grown up in industry and for which trade unions are partly responsible is receiving increasing criticism by the community at large. The two most overpaid groups are some top executives, who receive fantastic salaries that make little sense from the standpoint of stockholders since the government gets most of the last half of the salaries, and the semiskilled workers, who receive virtually the same wages as skilled workers (in some classifications, more than skilled workers) for jobs that require little training. For the overpayment of

---

[12] For an excellent discussion of the reasons for this shift, see George W. Brooks, "Reflections on the Changing Character of American Labor Unions," *Proceedings* of the Ninth Annual Meeting of the Industrial Relations Research Association, Cleveland, Ohio, 1956, pp. 33–43.

semiskilled workers, the trade unions must accept considerable responsibility. Trade unions also bear considerable responsibility for the widening spread between prices received by farmers and retail prices.

When teachers, librarians, scientists, government employees, young engineers, lawyers, doctors, other highly trained people, and farmers compare their earnings with the wages of workers on the assembly lines, no wonder they feel a sense of injustice. Part of the disfavor in which unions find themselves today results from their success in pushing the earnings of semiskilled workers too high relative to the earnings of many other kinds of workers.

Even more important has been the effect of unions on the movement of the general level of wages through time. During the past ten years, hourly compensation of employees in private industry outside of agriculture has increased more than twice as fast as the productivity of labor in all private industry outside of agriculture. A variety of conditions has caused wages to outrun productivity. One of these conditions has been the strong upward pressure of unions on wages in the principal manufacturing industries, construction, mining, and transportation. Indeed, the tendency of wages to outrun productivity, even in years of recession such as 1954, or in years of credit restraint, such as 1956 and 1957, cannot be satisfactorily explained except at least partly in terms of the upward pressure of trade unions on wages. Furthermore, unless the wage increases can be limited in general to increases in productivity, the price level must continue to rise.

The strong bargaining position of the unions creates a difficult dilemma for the leaders. If they fail to drive the best bargain they can, the members feel that the leaders are not faithfully representing them. If the leaders do drive the best possible bargain, they are bound to be blamed by the public for inflation—and the public is becoming increasingly impatient with wage increases that far outrun the growth in productivity. The president of the United States has asked employers and unions to avoid raising wages faster than the rise in productivity. The executive council of the AFL-CIO promptly issued a denial that price increases are closely related to wage increases.[13] But the problem of how to hold wage increases down to productivity increases remains unsolved, and until it is solved the country is bound to regard the wage policies of unions with considerable concern. It will not be safe for employers and union leaders to continue to ignore the demand that wage increases be limited to gains in productivity.

〈Some unions are strong enough to ignore the spirit of the public policy that workers are entitled to be represented by bargaining agents of their own choosing.〉These unions may seek to force workers to join unions which they do not care to join by organizing consumer boycotts or throwing picket lines around the place and cutting off supplies. In so doing, unions may not be violating the injunctions against "restraint" and "coercion," as the courts understand those terms. But the public of today is not prepared to tolerate these old-fashioned, rough-shod organizing methods. If unions wish additional restrictions on their activities, let them continue to use economic pressure to force people into unions that they do not wish to join.

---

[13] In the State of the Union Message of January 10, 1957, President Eisenhower said: "I urge leaders in business and labor to think well on their responsibilities to all the American people. . . . They owe the nation a vigilant guard against the inflationary tendencies that are always at work in a dynamic society operating at today's high levels—if our economy is to remain healthy, increases in wages and other labor benefits, negotiated by labor and management, must be reasonably related to improvements in productivity." *New York Times*, January 11, 1957, p. 10.

The AFL-CIO executive council, shortly after the president's message, denied the thesis that union wage policies had compelled price rises. The executive council said that the evidence shows that price pressures are "overwhelmingly unrelated to wage increases." *AFL-CIO News*, February 16, 1957, p. 4. The executive council said: "Excessive price increases in certain basic commodities have produced excessive profit margins in such key industries as auto and steel."

The strength of unions, plus strong sellers' markets, have caused a growth of corruption and racketeering in the labor movement. By and large, the standards of honesty in the trade-union movement are good. Nevertheless, the success of unions has attracted a growing number of racketeers into the movement, and, in addition, corruption has resulted from the temptations offered union officers by insurance companies and agencies eager to get union business, by the temptations presented by large insurance funds that some union officers have been administering, and by the opportunities for shakedown and extortion resulting from strong unions operating in sellers' markets. Racketeering and corruption are an extremely important problem to unions, as the leaders well know, because suspicion of corruption and racketeering greatly reduces the capacity of unions to attract members. But corruption and racketeering are only one facet of the central problem of the position of unions in the community. The central problem stems from the fact that trade unions have become so pervasive and so important that they are clothed with a public interest. Hence, the public is concerned, not simply that the trade unions be administered honestly, but that their activities and policies have regard for the public interest as well as for the interest of the members.

Finally, the economic success of trade unions and the exposure of corruption have diminished the popularity of unions and impaired to some extent the public relations of the labor movement. One can only speculate concerning the relative importance of these two causes. The exposure of corruption is the more dramatic cause, but great economic power seems invariably to arouse distrust on the part of the public. Business has had this experience, and now trade unions are having it. The economic power of trade unions will affect public attitudes toward them long after corruption has been eliminated.

Possible evidence of the decline in the public favor of trade unions is found in the falling percentage of votes received by trade unions in NLRB elections—though various special circumstances affect the decline.[14] Unions still win a

---

[14] Among the special influences are the fact that in the first years of the government's new labor policy the people who were most desirous of being organized joined unions and that those who remained outside were persons who for one reason or other did not feel the need of organizing. On the other hand, the success of unions in improving working conditions has apparently stirred up little demand for organization. The plants being organized today are smaller and probably less prosperous than the plants which were being organized a few years ago. (In 1949–50 the average number of votes in NLRB elections was 139; in 1956–57, it was 87. Back in 1936–37 it was 516, and in 1939–40 it was 447.) Employers in small plants are closer to their workers, and many of the employees may fear that stiff union demands will threaten the security of their jobs. The following are the figures on votes cast for and against unions in NLRB elections in recent years:

Fiscal year or years	Total	Votes cast for union	Per cent of total	Votes cast against unions	Per cent of total
1935–1939	692,509	569,092	82.2	123,417	17.8
1939–1943	3,455,826	2,844,023	82.3	611,803	17.7
1943–1947	3,470,638	2,686,731	77.4	783,907	22.6
1949–1950	781,382	649,432	83.1	131,950	16.9
1952–1953	639,739	497,286	77.7	142,453	22.3
1953–1954	449,673	314,701	70.0	134,972	30.0
1954–1955	453,442	335,393	74.0	118,049	26.0
1955–1956	414,568	268,531	64.8	146,037	35.2
1956–1957	410,619	261,762	63.7	148,857	36.3

The proportion of elections won by unions is shown in the following table:

Fiscal year or years	Total	Won by Unions	Per cent of total	Lost by Unions	Per cent of total
1935–1939	2,194	1,791	81.6	403	18.4
1939–1943	12,125	10,264	84.7	1,861	15.3
1943–1947	22,140	17,701	80.0	4,439	20.0
1949–1950	5,619	4,186	74.5	1,433	25.5
1952–1953	6,056	4,350	71.9	1,700	28.1
1953–1954	4,663	3,060	65.6	1,603	34.4
1954–1955	4,215	2,849	67.6	1,366	32.4
1955–1956	4,946	3,230	65.3	1,716	34.7
1956–1957	4,729	2,942	62.2	1,787	37.8

Note.—Covers representation elections requested by a union or other candidate for employee representative or by the employer.

Source: *NLRB Annual Reports:* 1957, p. 172; 1956, p. 175; 1955, p. 171; 1954, p. 166; 1953, p. 104; 1950, p. 232; 1947, p. 89.

majority of the NLRB elections and obtain a majority of the total votes cast, but the percentage of elections won and of votes received by unions has fallen sharply since 1950. The percentage of elections won by unions has dropped from 74.5 in 1950 to 67.6 in 1955 and to 62.2 in 1957, and the number of prounion votes has dropped from 83.1 per cent in 1950 to 74.0 per cent in 1955, and to 63.7 per cent in 1957.

VI

I have described the general reëxamination of unions, their activities, and their place in the economy that began more than ten years ago as one of the two most important facts about current industrial relations in the United States. This reëxamination, as I have pointed out, is being done by the unions themselves, by the government, by business managements, and by scholars. Some of it is friendly and has the purpose of helping unions adjust themselves to changing conditions; some of it is hostile and is designed to weaken unions. No one can review these developments without being impressed with the large amount of action that has occurred. The following are some of the principal developments:

Federal Legislation.—By far the most important federal legislation is the Taft-Hartley Act of 1947. The Taft-Hartley Act may be regarded as a logical follow-up of the Wagner Act. It retains the essential features of the Wagner Act, but to the aim of encouraging collective bargaining it adds the aim of giving some protection to employers, other unions, union members, and individuals against abuses of trade-union power. The Taft-Hartley Act is in need of strengthening. Of its many important provisions, the following stand out:

a. The law prohibits labor organizations by use of restraint or coercion from depriving employees of their right to bargain through representatives of their own choosing or of their right to remain unorganized.

b. It undertakes to protect employers and certified unions against strikes or boycotts intended to force the employer to bargain with a noncertified union.
c. It outlaws the closed shop, which means prohibiting unions from depriving nonmembers of a fair chance to make a living. And although the Act permits the union shop, it deprives unions of the right to compel the discharge of men who are willing to pay their dues.
d. It limits (though somewhat ineffectively) the right of unions to conscript neutrals in labor disputes.

State Legislation.—In the years immediately following the Wagner Act, many states passed laws applying the principles of the Wagner Act to intrastate commerce. Of late years, however, states have been more interested in legislation limiting the freedom of action of unions. The two principal state laws have been the Wisconsin Employment Peace Act, passed in 1939, before the general reëxamination of the position of unions, and the Massachusetts Act of 1947. The Wisconsin Act is significant because it was passed with the support of the farmers who had been allies of the trade unions on many issues but who split with them when the farmers decided that trade unions were becoming too powerful. In some respects, the Wisconsin law anticipated the Taft-Hartley Act. It does not outlaw the closed shop, but it substantially limits its use; it restricts the use of secondary boycotts; and it restricts other practices of unions that are deemed unfair labor practices. The Massachusetts Act does not prohibit the closed shop, but does give union members protection against arbitrary deprivation of membership.

In recent years many states have passed so-called right-to-work laws, and the prospect is that more of these laws will be passed. Although these laws have been sponsored by active antiunion interests, they have been passed in too many states and against too strong opposition to be interpreted as anything less than an expression of a broad popular belief in some parts of the country that the federal government has gone too far in encouraging unions. In particular, "right-to-work" laws mean that trade unions must pay much more attention to persuading people to join rather than forcing people in by short-cut methods.

Several states in recent years have passed legislation looking to the protection of the health-and-welfare funds of union members.

No-raiding Pacts by Various National Unions.—Unions have acted vigorously since 1949 to control union rivalries by antiraiding pacts. These have been of several kinds. The earliest were agreements between two unions, such as the agreement between the UAW and the Machinists originally made in 1949; and the agreement between the Machinists and the Teamsters made in 1953.[15] In 1951 the CIO set up an agreement governing organizational disputes arising from either organizing campaigns or raiding; in 1954 the AFL set up an internal-disputes plan applying to interunion disputes arising from organizing, raiding, and some work jurisdictional disputes; in 1953 and 1954 the AFL and the CIO made a no-raiding agreement.

On the whole, the no-raiding pacts probably tend to promote better trade-union government, because they reduce the effectiveness of threats of local unions to leave the national union when the national adopts policies that the locals do not like. But the no-raiding pacts increase the need for arrangements by which local unions can get a sympathetic consideration of their troubles. There are a number of misplaced locals which cannot get proper service except by transferring from one national to another. The labor movement has not yet developed an effective and orderly way of arranging for such transfers. I have in mind, for example, a local in the Steelworkers Union

---

[15] Dunlop, in his excellent analysis of agreements between national unions, 1949 to 1956, lists eleven no-raiding agreements between pairs of national unions. "Structural Changes in the American Labor Movement and Industrial Relations System," *Proceedings* of the Ninth Annual Meeting, Industrial Relations Research Association, Cleveland, Ohio, 1956, pp. 18 and 19.

in a multiplant company making electrical goods, in which the Steelworkers have no other locals. There is strong sentiment in the local for a transfer to one of the electrical-workers unions, but under the present rules of the AFL-CIO, such a transfer cannot be effected without the consent of the Steelworkers.

AFL and CIO Merger.—By far the most notable step in dealing with the problem of union rivalry created by the government's policy of encouraging collective bargaining was the merger of the AFL and CIO that was ultimately consummated in December, 1955. The merger provided that jurisdiction actually held by each affiliate at the time of the merger was to be preserved. With respect to unorganized workers, the provisions are somewhat indefinite, since the constitution provides that "each such affiliate shall retain and enjoy the same organizing jurisdiction in this federation which it had enjoyed by reason of its prior affiliation." The main reliance of the new federation for controlling union rivalries rests on the no-raiding agreements.

Expulsion of the International Longshoremen's Association. —On September 22, 1953, the AFL took a historic step in revoking the sixty-year-old charter of the International Longshoremen's Association. This was the first international affiliate to be expelled for corruption and racketeering—though the AFL once removed the officers of the old International Union of Mine, Mill, and Smelter Workers and appointed a receiver to reorganize the union. But the AFL did not lift a finger when gangsters put in their "tool" as president of the International Alliance of Theatrical Stage Employees in 1934, and the AFL had nothing to do with the ridding of this union from racketeers a few years later. Nor did the AFL raise a little finger against the domination of the Building Service Employees International Union by Scalise and the Capone mob or against notorious corruption at the international level in the Union of Operating Engineers. Unfortunately, the effort of the federation to provide the longshoremen with a new union free from corruption and gangsters failed by a small margin to win a majority of the longshoremen of New York.

Investigations by Committees of Congress and Legislatures. —The most notable are those of the Douglas Committee and the McClellan Committee, but the investigations of the New York Crime Commission in 1952–53 were important. These investigations, although of great significance, were of limited scope because they concentrated upon corruption and racketeering and paid little attention to problems raised by the normal activities of trade unions.

Changes in Internal Government by a Few Unions.—Some national unions have sought to protect themselves against corruption and antidemocratic influences by changes in their constitutions or their procedures. Some of the most important changes antedated the recent reëxamination of the position of trade unions. For example, the elaborate procedures for protecting union members charged with infractions of union rules developed by the Upholsterers' International Union go back to the 'twenties, though the procedures have been modified and simplified. In 1953 the Upholsterers' Union established the first independent citizens' appeal board empowered to review union internal trials and disciplinary actions. Four years later, the United Automobile Workers amended its constitution to authorize the Public Review Board with respect to union disciplinary actions.

The International Woodworkers of America drafted a new constitution, to be submitted to a special convention early in 1958, which would consolidate thirteen district councils into regions based on "geographic, economic, administrative, and contractual aspects." [16] The convention authorizing the drafting of the constitution also proposed that all unions adopt a "bill of rights" to insure safeguards against corrupt practices, including audit reports on finances and on health-and-welfare funds.

---

[16] *Monthly Labor Review* (November, 1957), p. 1384.

The Steelworkers Executive Board in July, 1957, adopted a stiff code of ethical practices that is binding on the International and its officers.[17]

Enforcement of Standards of Ethical Practices.—One objective of the AFL-CIO is the protection of the trade-union movement from corrupt and antidemocratic influences. Indeed, this objective is embodied in the constitution of the new federation.[18] The establishment of a Committee on Ethical Practices to assist the Executive Council in keeping the federation free from corruption and Communist influences is provided for in the constitution itself. Furthermore, at the first convention of the new federation in December, 1955, a strong resolution was adopted calling on the affiliated unions to take whatever steps may be necessary (including constitutional changes and changes in internal administrative procedures) to effect the policies and ethical standards set forth in the constitution of the AFL-CIO. The new constitution and the policies of the new federation are considerable departures from the principle of autonomy that guided the old AFL.

The AFL-CIO Executive Council has approved a code of ethical practices. The code at present consists of six parts relating to local union chapters: health-and-welfare funds; racketeers, crooks, Communists, and Fascists; investments and business interests of union officials; financial practices and proprietary activities of unions; and union democratic processes. Parts of this code might well be used as guides of conduct by business management.

In June, 1956, the Executive Council delegated authority to the Ethical Practices Committee to "initiate investigations of wrong-doing in labor's ranks." The Ethical Practices Committee conducted hearings pertaining to six unions, based upon exposures by Congressional committees, and presented reports to the Executive Council criticizing the six unions. The officials

---

[17] *Monthly Labor Review* (July, 1957), p. 856.
[18] See Article II, Sec. 10, Article VIII, Sec. 7, and Article 13, Sec. I (d).

of the six unions were asked to present their cases before the
Executive Council. Three unions, the Laundry Workers, the
Teamsters, and the Bakers, refused to meet the standards of
the Executive Council and were first suspended and then expelled by the convention of the AFL-CIO in December, 1957.
Three other unions, the Allied Industrial Workers, the Dis-
tillery Workers, and the United Textile Workers, agreed to a
cleanup under the surveillance of a monitor appointed by the
federation, and were put on probation. In two of these cases
the probation has been lifted because the terms required by
the federation have been met.

The efforts of the federation to enforce its code of ethical
practices and its willingness to expell powerful unions to
achieve this purpose merits strong approval. Two principal
questions remain unanswered. One is whether the federation,
without the help of Congressional committees or other public
authorities, can make an effective investigation of wrong-
doing where suspicion exists; the other is whether expulsion
or the threat of expulsion is an effective sanction. There can
be no doubt, however, that the federation intends to keep the
trade-union movement free from corruption, racketeering, and
antidemocratic practices, and that it will show resourcefulness
and determination in pursuing these purposes.

VII

Much less dramatic than the general examination of the trade-
union movement that has been going on during the past ten
years has been the progress that is being made by unions and
employers in adapting themselves to each other and in developing stable and reasonably satisfactory relations in most
enterprises. This progress has been mainly accomplished
through better administration of union-management contracts.
For this progress both unions and managements are responsible. Some managements from the very start adopted the only

policy that will work in the long run—the policy of being fair but firm. That policy consists of conceding to the union and the employees the rights that the contract, fairly interpreted, gives them, but of conceding them no more and of not yielding to attempts by the men or the union to get more than the contract provides.

But many managements did not at first base their dealings with unions on carefully considered policies. Some created trouble for themselves by attempting to give less than their union contracts, fairly interpreted, called for. Others practiced a policy of appeasement. It is amazing how many companies that had been well managed adopted a policy of expediency— tolerating various kinds of direct action in the form of wildcat strikes, slowdowns, sickness epidemics, refusal to work overtime, lax time keeping, and allowing shop committees to roam the shops freely, challenging orders of foremen and stirring up grievances. When management pursues either a policy of militancy or a policy of appeasement, there is little that the union can do to promote adherence to the contract and good administration of its provisions.

Both the policy of militancy and the policy of appeasement resulted in high costs. Hence, a shift to the only workable policy, the policy of being fair but firm, is sooner or later inevitable. In the postwar years, particularly since the recession of 1949, the shift has occurred in many plants. Sometimes the shift entails a strike, because a shift from militancy to fairness may be misinterpreted by the union as a sign of weakness, and a shift from appeasement may be interpreted as an attempt to undermine the union. But once the union is convinced that the management intends to be fair but firm, the union usually responds by promoting orderly administration of the agreement.

The development of more experienced personnel would in itself have enabled unions to contribute to the better administration of agreements. But unions have supplemented experi-

ence with training. They have provided themselves with carefully selected national representatives (drawn in large part
from the ablest local representatives); they have provided
themselves at the national level with some full-time staff ex-
perts; they have coöperated in making special studies and investigations (such as the Coöperative Wage Study in the steel
industry and many job evaluation plans); and they helped develop in some plants special arrangements for meeting special
problems, such as the union time-study men found in a number
of plants. All in all, the progress in improving the administration of union-employer contracts in American industry during
the past ten years has been impressive. Both management
and employees in most plants today are able to get questions
concerning the application of the contract expeditiously decided by orderly processes, and in most plants both seem
agreed that the decisions on the whole are satisfactory. There
are no over-all figures on the resort to arbitration, but in most
companies appeals to arbitration are few. It is impossible to
say whether they are increasing, but both managements and
unions try hard to avoid arbitration.

The principal obstacle to the development of better adapta-
tion between unions and managements is over the terms of
new agreements. The negotiating process itself, far more wordy
and cumbersome than any other negotiations except possibly
those between the United States and Russia, is being improved.
Preparations are more thoroughly made and are presented in
a more orderly fashion than formerly. In a few cases, bargaining has been preceded by prenegotiation meetings that have
explored the general situation and have paved the way for
the later discussions. An important problem has been stiff
union demands that far exceed the rise in productivity in
nonagricultural industry as a whole. The tendency for such
demands to create bad relations has been mitigated by market
conditions which have permitted employers to pass on part
of the wage increases in the form of higher prices. The price

increases which have contributed to industrial peace in the plants have hurt the relations of both labor and employers with the public. Thus, labor finds itself in the position of having to pay for good relations with employers by accepting bad relations with the public.

VIII

I would like to conclude by summarizing the position of trade unions in the community. Their economic position—or the economic position of most of them—is very strong, too strong for their own good. But their membership and strength are confined to a limited part of the economy—to the blue-collar workers in manufacturing, construction, mining, transportation, communication. In trade and government and among white-collar workers generally, trade unions have small membership. Trade unions are a minority group in the community as a whole. There is no strong demand for organization among most of the unorganized workers—in fact, many of the white-collar people are afraid that they will be forced into unions against their will. The unions have not yet learned how to make most white-collar workers eager to become members.

The great economic strength of trade unions is accompanied by very limited political strength, and the political influence of unions seems to be diminishing rather than growing. Much of the community—the small-business men, the farmers, many of the technical and professional men, and many of the white-collar workers—regards unions as representing privileged workers, that is, workers who have succeeded in getting conditions that most employees do not enjoy. The growing feeling that trade unions represent a privileged group creates suspicion and hostility toward unions, is a major obstacle to organizing efforts, and limits the political influence of unions; but it does not create a strong urge to join the privileged group.

The position of unions in the community calls for important changes in some union policies and the more vigorous pursuit of other policies. Unions will find the public increasingly critical of wage increases that far exceed the rise in productivity. Unless unions curb the use of their economic power, they will make the public less and less sympathetic with their demands. This means that they will have to convince the members not to expect the unions to press for wage demands that exceed increases in productivity. Unions, of course, have not been used to doing this sort of thing. They have gone ahead on the totally unrealistic premise that the only limit to their wage demands need be their economic strength. That is not true. The public has been slow to demand that unions exercise moderation but, as time goes on, the public will become more hostile to demands that go far beyond the demonstrated average long-term rise in productivity.[19]

The position of unions in the community calls for a vigorous pursuit of the new policy of the AFL-CIO of ridding its affiliates of corruption, racketeering, and antidemocratic practices. There is no doubt that the leaders of the AFL-CIO understand the importance of achieving this result, and Mr. Hayes, the chairman of the Ethical Practices Committee, has expressed confidence in the ability of the federation to achieve it. But Mr. Hayes is unduly optimistic. The labor movement, especially the rank and file, must help clean up the trade unions, but assistance from the federal government is essential. The task is a formidable one and the need is imperative. The trade-union movement cannot afford to have its history during the next twenty-five years studded with episodes comparable to those associated with the names of George Browne, Willie Bioff, George Berry, William Maloney, George Scalise, Joseph P. Ryan, Joseph S. Fay, James Bove, John Possehl, Frank

---

[19] I think that the public will not be averse to demands that are mildly "unreasonable" on the grounds that management needs a spur to try to raise the rate of increase in productivity.

Brewster, James G. Cross, Dave Beck, the two DeKonings, Anthony Valente, Lloyd Klenert, and others. It is true that the corruption and racketeering have affected only a tiny fraction of the 16,000 full-time officers of American unions, but at one time or another in the past twenty-five years corrupt officials have headed at least ten international unions. This has shaken the confidence of the public in all unions.

The task of keeping out corruption is made more formidable by the fact that in some industries corruption in unions is simply part of a broader fabric of corruption that includes business practices and local political life. But to the extent that the labor movement is unable to eradicate serious corruption and racketeering from unions, the federal government will be compelled to exercise more and more supervision over the internal affairs of trade unions. The most difficult problem of the Committee on Ethical Practices is likely to be stimulating action by officers of national unions who are themselves free from corruption but who are unwilling to proceed against powerful local bosses in their own unions.

The greatest need of the trade-union movement is part of a broader need of American society as a whole—the need for objectives and ideals capable of enabling men to lead significant and satisfying lives. Ours is pretty much a civilization without a purpose—except that there is general agreement that the good life should be made available to all members of the community. But the problem of what is the good life receives little attention. Hence, men strive vigorously and successfully for more production without knowing, asking, or indeed caring what the more production is for. We lack significant social purposes. Trade unions also suffer from lack of adequate goals. So long as they were striving to establish a system of industrial jurisprudence in the plants and to give workers elementary rights and protection, they had a purpose that evoked idealism and that enabled men to live significant lives. Now that they have accomplished that important purpose and are simply bargaining to get a little more for men who already have much, they cease to have objectives capable of arousing men's devotion and idealism.

It has always been said that business unionism is the only kind of unionism that will work in the American environment, and that has probably been true. It may still be true, but one is compelled to doubt this conclusion. In the old days, when business unionism was getting established, it could command men's idealism while still remaining practical because merely getting union recognition was a great reform. Now success has put business unionism in the position where merely being practical prevents it from having adequate social objectives. Hence, unionism needs to transform itself—to escape the results of success by embracing new goals, by becoming a champion of new and better social and economic institutions than we now possess and by becoming an instrument for achieving these new and better institutions. Business unionism is not enough. Business unionism mixed with the aim of broad social reforms is needed.

ARCHIBALD COX

The Role of Law in Preserving Union Democracy

AN INQUIRY into the present and potential role of law in preserving union democracy requires a measuring stick—or at
least a point of view. My point of view results from a conception of the function of labor unions in an industrial community;
and it concerns an evaluation of the importance of certain
aspects of personal liberty.

The first function of labor unions is to substitute the economic power of group action for individual weakness in negotiating wages, hours, and other conditions of employment.

The second function is to secure a measure of job security.
This is partly an issue between the employees and the employer, but it also concerns competition among employees. The
job security which members of a closed union enjoy under
closed-shop contracts denies nonmembers equality of opportunity.

The third function is to extend the rule of law to industrial establishments. A collective-bargaining agreement defines
rights and duties. It substitutes rule for arbitrary power. A
grievance procedure terminating in arbitration provides a fair
and impartial forum for administering the law of the plant.

The fourth function of labor unions is to enable workers to
participate in the government of their industrial lives through

chosen representatives even as all of us may participate, through elected representatives, in political government. "So the union is formed to compel management to share governing power with the workers. Each worker seeks to participate in the planning of his own life or in the decisions which affect him, and the labor union is the institution which enables him to do so." [1]

A union governed by dictatorial officials might be able to perform the two economic functions as long as the members remain loyal and the public is tolerant. But an undemocratic union cannot fulfill the third and fourth functions. An individual worker gains no human rights by substituting an autocratic union officialdom for the tyranny of the boss. If two aims of collective bargaining are to extend the rule of law and to give individual employees a chance to recapture freedom and personal dignity by participating in decisions affecting their industrial lives, then there must be not only democracy within the labor movement but also safeguards protecting individuals and minorities against the oppression of officials and even of a numerical majority of the members. Only a democratic union, sensitive to the rights of minorities, can help men to achieve the ideals of individual responsibility, equality of opportunity, and self-determination.

Of course one might concede the importance of union democracy yet deny the usefulness of law as a means of achieving democracy. There are important reasons for believing that a heavy burden of persuasion rests upon those who deny the usefulness of law.

First, preserving union democracy often requires the protection of individuals and minorities against numerical majorities or an officialdom that acts with majority assent. In the United States we have not been willing to trust even govern-

---

[1] Katz, "Minimizing Disputes Through the Adjustment of Grievances," 12 *Law and Contemp. Prob.* 249, 251 (1947).

mental self-restraint in dealing with basic liberties. We rely
upon written constitutions enforced by an independent judi-
ciary. A private organization has no greater claim to untram-
meled power.

Second, labor unions play a more important role in the community than other private organizations. Their powers are
greater and their functions are different from those of a fraternal benefit association or social club. A corporation rarely
affects a shareholder to the same degree that the bargaining
representative influences the lives of employees in the bargaining unit.

Third, labor unions occupy their present position largely
by force of law. Under the National Labor Relations Act [2]
the union which acts as the bargaining representative has
power, in conjunction with the employer, to fix a man's wages,
hours, and conditions of employment without his assent. The
individual employee may not lawfully negotiate with his employer.[3] He is bound by the union contract.[4] As a matter of
practice, if not in legal theory, the union also controls the
grievance procedure where a man's contract rights are enforced.[5] The government which gives unions this power has

[2] 49 Stat. 449 (1935), as amended by 61 Stat. 136 (1947), 29. U.S.C.
§151 ff. (1952).
[3] *Medo Photo Supply Co. v. NLRB*, 321 U.S. 678 (1944); cf. *J. I. Case
Co. v. NLRB*, 321 U.S. 332 (1944).
[4] See *Steele v. Louisville & N.R.R.*, 323 U.S. 192, 202 (1944) where
Chief Justice Stone said on behalf of the Court: "Congress has seen fit to
clothe the bargaining representative with powers comparable to those
possessed by a legislative body both to create and restrict the rights of
those whom it represents."
[5] Compare *Terrell v. Local Lodge 758, International Association of
Machinists*, 150 ACA 23, 309 P.2d 130 (1957); *Garner v. KMTR Radio
Corp.*, 31 CCH Lab. Cas. par. 70,368 (Cal. Dist. Ct. of App. 1956);
Chacko v. Pittsburgh Steel Co., 40 Lab. Rel. Rep. 2366 (Pa. Ct. of Com.
Pleas, 1957); *Disanti v. United Glass and Ceramic Workers*, 40 Lab. Rel.
Rep. 2548 (Pa. Ct. of Com. Pleas, 1957); and *Mello v. United Steel
Workers*, 82 R.I. 60, 105 A.2d 806 (1954); with *Elgin, J. & E. Ry v.
Burley*, 325 U.S. 711 (1945), affirmed on rehearing, 327 U.S. 661
(1946); *Alabama Power Co. v. Haygood*, 95 S.2d 98 (Ala. 1957); and

the concomitant obligation to provide safeguards against abuse. The most effective safeguard is legal assurance that unions will be responsive to the desires of the men and women whom they represent.[6]

I do not mean to imply that there are no opposing considerations. The community would gain nothing from legislation which diminished the effectiveness of labor unions in order to make them democratic. It would gain nothing from legislation which impaired their independence of government. These are considerations which must be kept clearly in view in appraising both the present law and proposed legislation but they fall short of demonstrating any fundamental practical or philosophical objection to all regulation of internal union affairs. Indeed, it is the very belief in the importance of a strong and independent labor movement which motivates many of us who believe that there is need for legislation enforcing the basic fiduciary obligations resting upon union officials and guaranteeing a measure of internal democracy. In our judgment such laws, if soundly conceived, would strengthen the labor movement. They would remove a source of corruption which might ultimately weaken if not destroy; they would rebuild the confidence of union members as well as the general public; they would ward off the repressive laws which antiunion forces are awaiting the opportunity to press upon the Congress. And thus far, no one has shown how they would handicap any

---

Eversole v. La Combe. 125 Mont. 87, 231 P.2d 945 (1951). The former group of decisions is also supported by *dicta* in cases denying the employees the right to compel arbitration. Example, *United States v. Voges*, 124 F. Supp. 543 (E.D.N.Y. 1954); *Bianculli v. Brooklyn Union Gas Co.*, 19 Lab. Arb. Rep. 83, 85 (N.Y. Sup. Ct. 1952).

[6] The other source of protection is the implied statutory duty of the bargaining agent to represent every employee in the unit fairly and without hostile discrimination. It seems plain, however, that the courts can use this concept only to reach egregious unfairness such as racial discrimination. Closer scrutiny would interfere with free collective bargaining. For a general discussion of this subject, see Cox, "The Duty of Fair Representation," 2 *Villanova L. Rev.* 151 (1957).

union in collective bargaining or the pursuit of trade-union goals.[7]

One other general observation may be necessary to avoid misunderstanding. To talk about occasional instances of autocracy or oppression of individuals is not to criticize the entire labor movement. The labor movement as a whole is firmly dedicated to the democratic ideals concern for which led to the calling of this conference. Its commitment to freedom is stronger and more energetic than one finds in almost any other segment of the community. Consequently when we discuss ways and means of increasing democracy and preserving individual liberties within labor unions we are exploring ways of reaching what I take to be a common set of goals. Though the record be good, we should not shut our eyes to the chance for improvement.

ADMISSION AND EXPULSION OF MEMBERS [8]

Union practices and the law pertaining to the admission and expulsion of members are important in the attainment of freedom because:

[7] I am not impressed by the argument that laws guaranteeing democratic rights to union members are an insult to the overwhelming number of union officials who are sensitive to the rights of minorities and insist on fair procedures. None of us is offended by the laws against wife-beating even though we would not beat our wives in the absence of legislation. Should Congress have refrained from enacting the Securities Act because of the sensitivities of honest brokers?

[8] Among the valuable articles on this subject are Chafee, "The Internal Affairs of Associations Not for Profit," 43 *Harv. L. Rev.* 993 (1930); Aaron and Komaroff, "Statutory Regulations of Internal Union," 44 *Ill. L. Rev.* 425, 631 (1949); Summers, "The Right to Join a Union," 47 *Col. L. Rev.* 33 (1947); Summers, "Legal Limitations on Union Discipline," 64 *Harv. L. Rev.* 1049 (1951); Summers, "Disciplinary Powers of Unions," 3 *Ind. and Lab. Rel. Rev.* 483 (1950); "Disciplinary Procedures of Unions," 4 *ibid.* 15 (1950); Stone, "Wrongful Expulsion from Trade Unions," 34 *Can. Bar Rev.* 1111 (1956).

In discussing the present state of the law pertaining to union membership, elections, and receiverships I have tried to cite representative decisions on the main points but there is no effort to collect all the authorities or to cover the details fully.

First, the employee in the bargaining unit who is unfairly excluded from the union or who is denied the right to vote has no opportunity to participate in fixing his terms and conditions of employment. He is bound by the action of an organization in whose councils he has no vote. In his case it is a fraud to call collective bargaining an instrument of industrial democracy.

Second, expulsion may be used as a method of suppressing criticism of union policy.

Third, control over union membership can also be used to suppress individual liberty. The worker who can be a member of the United Automobile Workers for the purposes of collective bargaining while he actively supports the reëlection of Senator Goldwater would lose freedom if the UAW expelled members who engaged in political activities distasteful to a majority of the union, for in that event the worker would be forced to choose between avoiding the political activities and foregoing the opportunity to influence bargaining policies. Similarly a person loses liberty if he can be forced to choose between membership in a railway brotherhood and testifying against legislation espoused by the organization.

Expulsion.—The legal rules governing union membership originated in earlier decisions for religious organizations and social clubs, and somewhat later fraternal benefit associations. Judges were naturally reluctant to interfere in religious controversies or to force the members of a London Club to dine with a man who was personally obnoxious. But in time it became clear that expulsion from a voluntary association might result in the loss of substantial property rights, because each member owns an undivided share in the association's property, and sometimes membership carries a right to valuable insurance policies. The equity courts began to review expulsions in order to protect these property rights, and having taken jurisdiction on this ground, they went on to dispose of the whole controversy even to the point of reinstating an expelled member instead of confining themselves to awarding him the value of his property interest.[9]

The constitution and bylaws of a voluntary association are often said to be a contract between the members. Expulsion in violation of the constitution or bylaws would be a breach of contract; and breach of contract is a conventional ground for judicial intervention when it results in an injury cognizable by law. To get the injury one would logically have to fall back on the theory of a property interest in the union assets, but the point was sometimes overlooked.[10] The contract theory also had a logical fallacy. The theory justifies nothing more than enforcement of the constitution and bylaws, yet for many years the courts have set aside expulsion that conformed to the union constitutions but violated the court's conception of "natural justice." [11]

Scholars dissatisfied with the property and contract theories have argued that union membership is an advantageous relationship, which the law should protect against unjustified interferences.[12] Just as it is wrong—a tort—to interfere, without justification, in the relationship between man and wife, parent and child, or a merchant and his customers, so, the argument runs, it is a wrong to interfere improperly in the relation between a union member and the union. This theory has little support outside academic circles,[13] but it is a potential source of growth in developing legal protection of the worker's

---

[9] For example, *Spayd v. Ringing Rock Lodge,* 270 Pa. 67, 113 Atl. 70 (1921).

[10] "In sound logic the presence of the contract affords no basis for relief unless we are ready to abandon the traditional limitation of equity jurisdiction to property rights, as we ought to do." Chafee, *op. cit.* (n. 8), at 1002. But possibly the contract of membership is "property" enough.

[11] *Gilmore v. Palmer,* 109 Misc. 552, 179 N.Y. Supp. 1 (Sup. Ct. 1919); *Spayd v. Ringing Rock Lodge,* 270 Pa. 67, 113 Atl. 70 (1921).

[12] Chafee, *op. cit.* (n. 8); Pound, "Equitable Relief against Defamation and Injuries to Property," 29 *Harv. L. Rev.* 640, 677–681 (1916).

[13] The leading judicial opinion embracing this view is *Tunney v. Orchard* (1955), 15 W.W.R. (N.S.). 49 (1955), 3 D.L.R. 15 (G. A. Man).

interest in becoming a member of a labor union, because the
contract and property theories are applicable only to expulsions.[14] Obviously the applicant for membership has no property rights in the union's assets and no contract with the members.

Before he may challenge the union's action in court, an expelled member must show either that he has exhausted all
remedies by appeal within the organization or else that the
internal remedies are inadequate.[15] The rule is enforced with
varying degrees of rigor. Some courts refused to intervene because the plaintiff had not appealed to the union convention
to be held in another city two or three years later,[16] but under
the modern trend resort to the convention is seldom required.[17]
There is also considerable room for judicial discretion in ex-
cusing an appeal to the General Executive Board on the
ground that the union officialdom has prejudged the case.[18]
On some occasions, I suspect, the exhaustion-of-remedies doctrine has prevented expelled members from obtaining effective
relief against injustice simply because cost and delay are on
the side of the defendants, but surely the rule is necessary
despite its faults. Outside bodies, whether courts, administrative agencies, or private independent appeal boards should not
interfere in the internal affairs of a labor organization until the
organization has had a reasonable opportunity to correct any
mistakes committed or injustice done by subordinate bodies.
It is in this way that independent self-government is maintained.

---

[14] See pp. 50 f.

[15] A general discussion of this doctrine may be found in Vorenburg,
"Exhaustion of Intra-Union Remedies as a Condition Precedent to Appeal
to the Courts," 2 *Lab. L.J.* 487 (1951).

[16] *Mulcahy v. Huddell*, 272 Mass. 539, 172 N.E. 796 (1930); *Snay v.
Lovely*, 276 Mass. 159, 176 N.E. 791 (1931).

[17] *Gleeson v. Conrad*, 81 N.Y.S.2d 368 (1948).

[18] Compare *Reilly v. Hogan*, 32 N.Y.S.2d 864 (Sup. Ct. 1942) and
Corregan v. Hay, 94 App. Div. 71, 87 N.Y. Supp. 956 (4th Dept. 1949)
with *Hall v. Morrin*, 293 S.W.2d 435 (Mo. App. 1927) and *Fish v. Huddell*, 51 F.2d 319 (D.C. Cir. 1931).

None of the theories determines the standards that the courts should apply in reviewing the expulsion of a union member. The familiar formula is that the discipline must be set aside if it is inconsistent with the union constitution or by-laws, or contrary to natural justice. The actual decisions show that the courts will set the expulsion of a member aside upon any of several grounds: that the procedure violated the constitution and bylaws; [19] that the ground of expulsion alleged was not within the constitution or bylaws; [20] that the procedure, although it conformed to the union's constitution and bylaws, did not afford the member a fair hearing; [21] that the expulsion, although it conformed to the union's constitution and bylaws, was on grounds contrary to natural justice—a euphemism for "contrary to public policy"; [22] and that the expulsion was in bad faith because the purported ground was only a pretense for getting rid of a troublesome member.[23]

The last three grounds concern us most because they establish the minimum legal safeguards for a worker's union membership.

The legal rule invalidating expulsion without a hearing requires observance of much the same minimum safeguards as the court imposes upon the state and federal governments in the name of due process of law. The accused member must

---

[19] *Harris v. National Union of Marine Cooks and Stewards*, C.A.2d, 221 P.2d 136 (1950); *Walsh v. Reardon*, 274 Mass. 530, 174 N.E. 912 (1931); *Howland v. Local Union 306, UAW-CIO*, 323 Mich. 305, 35 N.W.2d 166 (1948); *Savard v. Industrial Trades Union*, 76 R.I. 496, 72 A.2d 660 (1950).

[20] *Otto v. Journeymen Tailors' J. and B. Union*, 75 Cal. 308, 17 Pac. 217 (1888).

[21] *Gilmore v. Palmer*, 109 Misc. 552, 179 N.Y. Supp. 1 (Sup. Ct. 1919). *Contra:* State ex rel. *Dame v. Le Fevre*, 251 Wis. 146, 28 N.W.2d 349 (1947).

[22] *Spayd v. Ringing Rock Lodge*, 270 Pa. 67, 113 Atl. 70 (1921).

[23] *Otto v. Journeymen Tailors' P. and B. Union.* 75 Cal. 308, 17 Pac. 217 (1888); *Fleming v. Motion Picture Machine Operators*, 1 A.2d 850 (1938) affirmed 124 N.J. Eq. 269, 1 A.2d 386 (1939); *Kuzych v. White* (1950) 4 D.L.R. 187 (C.A.B.C.); cf. *Eshman v. Huebner*, 226 Ill. App. 537 (1922).

be given an opportunity to hear the charge,[24] to present evidence in his defense,[25] and to confront and probably cross-examine the witnesses against him.[26] If there is a trial body it must be impartial; it may not include his accusers.[27] Presumably a trial could be held before the full membership.[28] Sometimes the question is raised whether a member has a right to legal counsel in aid of his defense. I am not aware of any square decisions on the point but personally I doubt whether the courts would or should enforce so rigid a requirement. The member is entitled to be put upon a roughly equal footing with the prosecutors. If they are laymen, then surely he is entitled to no more than lay assistance. Granted that union officers are usually more skilled than the defendants in parliamentary law and other rules of procedure, there would be a disproportionate loss in self-government if the trial of charges of misconduct were turned over to professional advocates.

It is more difficult to draw a line between permissible grounds of expulsion and grounds that the law regards inadequate despite the constitution and bylaws. Here the law grows slowly through case-by-case decisions. A member may be expelled for strikebreaking,[29] for working at wages below the

[24] *Armant v. Cannon Employees Association* 11 Lab. Rel. Rep. 752 (Cal. Super. 1942) (Barred from knowing evidence against him); *Bartone v. Di Pietro,* 18 N.Y.S.2d 178 (Sup. Ct. 1939) (no notice of nature of charge); *Walsh v. International Alliance of Theatrical Stage Employees,* 22 N.J. Misc. 161, 37 A.2d 667 (1944) (charge too vague).
[25] *Cotton Jammers' and Longshoremen's Association v. Taylor,* 23 Tex. Civ. App. 367, 56 S.W. 553 (1900); *People ex rel. Holmstrom v. Independent Dock Builders' Benevolent Union,* 164 App. Div. 267, 149 N.Y. Supp. 771 (1st Dept. 1914).
[26] *Armant v. Cannon Employees Association,* 11 Lab. Rel. Rep. 752 (Cal. Sup. Ct. 1942); *Brooks v. Engar,* 259 App. Div. 333, 19 N.Y.S.2d 114 (1st Dept. 1940); *Fales v. Musicians' Protective Union,* 40 R.I. 34, 99 Atl. 823 (1917).
[27] *Gaestel v. Brotherhood of Painters,* 120 N.J. Eq. 358, 185 Atl. 36 (1936); *Coleman v. O'Leary,* 58 N.Y.S.2d 812 (Sup. Ct. 1945); cf. *Cohen v. Rosenburg,* 262 App. Div. 274, 27 N.Y.S.2d 834 (1st Dept. 1941).
[28] *Dragwa v. Federal Labor Union,* 136 N.J. Eq. 172, 41 A.2d 32 (1945). *Contra: Reilly v. Hogan,* 32 N.Y.S.2d 864 (Sup. Ct. 1942).
[29] *Becker v. Calnan,* 313 Mass. 625, 48 N.E.2d 668 (1943); *Havens v. King,* 221 App. Div. 475, 224 N.Y. Supp. 193 (3rd Dept. 1927).

union scale,[30] or for aiding an employer to obtain an injunction
against a strike.[31] But a member of a licensing board cannot
lawfully be expelled by his union because his official activities
displease it,[32] nor may a union expel a member for testifying
against it under oath in an arbitration proceeding [33] or appear-
ing before a legislative committee as an individual in opposition to bills sponsored by the union.[34] The familiar provision
in union constitutions which states that bringing suit against
the union is ground for expulsion, is plainly invalid.[35] There
is a nice factual line to be drawn between legitimate criticism,
which is an exercise of the privilege of free speech and will
not justify expulsion, and stirring up dissension within the union, which is a justification.[36]

Possibly one can generalize by saying that expulsion is permitted for conduct endangering normal trade-union objectives,
but that the courts will set aside expulsions where the alleged
misconduct consisted of the performance of a civic duty or the
exercise of personal civil liberties. The generalization leaves
difficult problems unsolved especially in the realm of political
action. Some years ago Cecil B. DeMille was expelled by the
American Federation of Radio Artists for refusing to pay one
dollar assessed upon union members in a drive to raise funds
to defeat a so-called right-to-work law proposed in a California

[30] Cf. *O'Keefe v. Local 463 of the United Association of Plumbers and Gasfitters*, 277 N.Y. 300, 14 N.E.2d 77 (1938); *Schmidt v. Rosenburg* 49 N.Y.S.2d 364 (Sup. Ct. 1944).

[31] *Burke v. Monumental Div.*, No. 52, B.L.E., 286 Fed. 949 (D. Md. 1922).

[32] *Schneider v. Local Union No. 60, United Association of Journeymen Plumbers*, 116 La. 270, 40 So. 700 (1905).

[33] Cf. *A. Angrisani v. Stearn*, 167 Misc. 731, 3 N.Y.S.2d 701 (Sup. Ct. 1938); *Thompson v. Brotherhood of Locomotive Engineers*, 41 Tex. Civ. App. 176 (1905); Link-Belt Speeder Corp., 2 Lab. Arb. Rep. 338 (1945).

[34] *Abdon v. Wallace*, 95 Ind. App. 604, 165 N.E. 68 (1929); *Spayd v. Ringing Rock Lodge*, 270 Pa. 67, 113 Atl. 70 (1921).

[35] *Burke v. Monumental Div.*, No. 52, B.L.E., 273 Fed. 707; see *Trailmobile Co. v. Whirls*, 331 U.S. 40, 69 (1947) (Jackson, J. dissenting).

[36] See Summers, 64 *Harv. L. Rev.* pp. 1069–1071, 1074.

referendum. The Supreme Court of California refused to set the expulsion aside.[37] Not many tears will be shed over Cecil B. DeMille's one-dollar bill, but the case raised some nice theoretical questions which grow still harder with each twist of the facts. Do monetary assessments ever raise questions of civil liberty? Suppose that the San Francisco local of the United Brotherhood of Carpenters levied a five-dollar assessment upon each member in order to build up a fund to be spent in electing Attorney General Brown as governor. Might a lifelong Republican be required to pay the assessment under penalty of expulsion? Or suppose that a union member was expelled for personal activity in support of a so-called right-to-work law. Is this a form of treason to the union or an exercise of political freedom that the union may not compel him to forego as the price of taking part in its economic activities? These questions cannot be answered simply by invoking majority rule because the very question at issue is whether the individual or minority should not be guaranteed this degree of political liberty regardless of the will of the majority, just as the Constitution guarantees religious liberty and freedom of speech against political majorities. One must balance the value of allowing all workers the opportunity both to participate in collective bargaining and also to exercise complete political freedom against the value of allowing men and women who constitute a majority in the union to confine their association to like-minded people. The choice is not easy.

I hesitate to predict the course of judicial decision upon these doubtful issues. For our purposes two comments are probably sufficient. First, in my opinion the common-law rules evolved by judges furnish adequate theoretical protection against unjust expulsion from a labor union. Second, although this body of law is still in the course of evolution, there are

---

[37] *DeMille v. American Federation of Radio Artists*, 31 Cal.2d 139, 187 P.2d 769 (1947), cert. denied 333 U.S. 876 (1948).

sufficient principles to guide the courts or an administrative agency in resolving future cases.

It is more doubtful whether the present law affords a practical remedy. Workers hesitate to bring suit against a labor union. The money stakes are small. The legal questions are likely to be difficult. Several dilatory defenses are available to the union. Under such circumstances time and cost are serious practical barriers to obtaining effective relief. If legislation is needed to deal with expulsions, it should be aimed at these obstacles rather than the basic postulates of substantive law.

Admission.—The present law is much less favorable to the individual worker who believes that he has been unfairly denied admission to a labor union. The black-letter rule is that no one has a legally protected right to become a member of a voluntary association. Consequently a union may exclude an applicant for any reason, good or bad, or for no reason.[38]

It seems unlikely that the courts will change the rule just stated. The rule has been recited so many times that it has a stronger ring of authority than the precedents actually warrant. The property and contract theories which are invoked to sustain judicial review of expulsions cannot logically be stretched to cover an unfair denial of admission. Yet there are three lines of thought any one of which a strong court might follow if it were persuaded that the public interest required it to make new law upon the subject.

1) One course would be to recognize that the individual worker has a sufficient interest in the membership of the bargaining representative to merit legal protection. Unions exercise powers under the National Labor Relations and Railway Labor acts which are far greater than the powers of other voluntary associations—greater indeed than the powers unions

---

[38] 87 C.J.S., Trade Unions § 33 (1954). But the modern view denies a union the privilege of enforcing closed-shop contracts against those to whom it arbitrarily denies admission. *James v. Marinship Corp.*, 25 Cal.2d 721, 155 P.2d 329 (1944).

exercised before the legislation. Union membership is corre-
spondingly more important. This factor distinguishes earlier
cases and furnishes the ground for legal recognition of the interest and the creation of tort liability for unjustified interference.[39] Furthermore, union membership today rarely means
the close personal association that must have influenced the
courts in their reluctance to compel social clubs and religious
organizations to admit unwanted members.[40]

2) The bargaining representative is under an implied statutory duty to represent every member of the bargaining unit
fairly and without hostile discrimination.[41] The duty is difficult to enforce except in blatant cases of racial discrimination.[42] Might it not be said that performance of the duty requires admitting all members of the bargaining unit to union
membership (unless there is a just cause for excluding them)
because membership is the best assurance that a man's voice
will be heard and his interests represented? There is faint support for this view in Justice Stone's statement that "the union is
required to consider requests of nonunion members of the
craft and expressions of their views with respect to collective
bargaining with the employer and to give them notice of and
opportunity for hearing upon its proposed action," [43] because
the union meeting is the normal place to be heard; but in another passage the justice stated his opinion that nothing in the
statute lessened a union's freedom in choosing its members.[44]

3) It has also been argued that the powers which the NLRA

[39] Cf. *Raevsky v. Upholsterers' International Union of North America,*
38 Pa. D. & C. 187, 195 (1940); *Dusing v. Nuzzo,* 177 Misc. 35, 37, 29
N.Y.S.2d 882, 884 (Sup. Ct. 1941), modified and affirmed 263 App.
Div. 59, 37 N.Y.S.2d 750 (3d Dept. 1941).
[40] Compare the erosion of the old rule that equity would never enforce
a contract of employment. Cf. *Phelps Dodge Corp. v. NLRB,* 313 U.S.
177 (1941).
[41] *Steele v. Louisville and N.R. Co.,* 323 U.S. 192 (1944).
[42] For a general discussion of the duty, see Cox, "The Duty of Fair
Representation," 2 *Villanova L. Rev.* 151 (1957).
[43] 323 U.S. at 204.
[44] *Ibid.*

and RLA vest in labor unions are so far governmental that all their actions, including the election and rejection of members, are subject to the restrictions that the Fifth and Fourteenth amendments impose on the federal and state authorities.[45] This view would provide legal relief against admission policies which discriminated upon grounds of race, creed, or color. One state court appears to have accepted the argument [46] but it has been rejected elsewhere.[47] In my opinion the reasoning is highly dangerous. The implications of calling labor unions the instrumentalities of government are not easy to perceive, but surely the designation would invite more regulation with consequent loss of independence.

Proposed Legislation.—There is no major bill pending in the present Congress which would protect the interest of individual workers in acquiring or retaining union membership. Representative Jacobs sponsored such a bill some years ago.[48] Another was prepared by the American Civil Liberties Union.[49] The McClellan committee apparently found no need for the protection, but it did not survey the present law either, nor did it investigate current practices.[50]

In my judgment the need is not very great for those who are already union members because the present law affords them protection if they will but invoke it. The need is great for employees who are unfairly denied admission to a labor union. It is no answer to say that unfair exclusions do not take place very often. The purpose of many laws is to compel a few wrongdoers to live up to the standards observed by society as

---

[45] Rauh, "Civil Rights and Liberties and Labor Unions," 8 *Lab. L.J.* 874 (1957).

[46] *Betts v. Easely,* 161 Kan. 459, 169 P.2d 831 (1946).

[47] *Oliphant v. Brotherhood of Locomotive Firemen and Enginemen,* 156 F. Supp. 89, cert. denied 355 U.S. 893 (1957); *Ross v. Ebert,* 275 U.S. 523, 81 N.W.2d 315 (1957).

[48] H.R. 4914, 81st Cong. 1st sess. (1949).

[49] The A.C.L.U. bill is analyzed in Aaron and Komaroff, "Statutory Regulations of Union Affairs," 44 *Ill. L. Rev.* 631 (1949).

[50] S. Rep. No. 1417, 85th Cong. 2d sess.

a whole. And if new legislation is to provide a remedy against
unfair exclusion of applicants for membership, it should also
eliminate the practical obstacles to effective review of expulsions.

It would seem relatively simple to prepare legislation fur-
nishing the necessary safeguards. The statute should impose
the following limitations on the power of expulsion or deprivation of voting rights: [51]

1) The union must follow its own constitution and bylaws.
This standard is applied by the courts today.

2) There must be a fair trial, including an opportunity to
hear the evidence, to present opposing evidence, to have a disinterested trial body and the other essentials of due process
of law. This requirement is also one developed by the common
law.

3) The expulsion should not be "inconsistent with established public policy." As noted above, the common-law courts
have already indicated concepts of public policy which may
invalidate an expulsion even though there was full compliance
with the union constitution. The agency applying this standard
would start with these existing decisions and develop new particular applications in the same way that the common law
has grown for centuries. Congress followed an analogous
course when it required the Federal Trade Commission to
give meaning to the statutory phrase "unfair methods of competition," [52] and the National Labor Relations Board to decide
what was a refusal "to bargain collectively." [53]

4) An expulsion should also be invalid if it is "not warranted
by the offense, if any, committed by the employee against the
labor organization." This requirement would partly duplicate
the third standard. The immediate aim is to prevent expulsions

---

[51] The suggested standards are taken from a Massachusetts statute
granting such protection to employees subject to a closed or union-shop
agreement. General Laws, c. 150A, §§ 4, 6A.

[52] Federal Trade Commission Act, § 5, 15 U.S.C. § 45.

[53] NLRA 8 (a)(5), 8 (b)(3), 8 (d).

which are discriminatory or so obviously based on trivial offenses as to suggest arbitrariness or bad motives. The standard is analogous to the now familiar rule in collective-bargaining agreements that forbids an employer to discharge an employee "without just cause." Arbitrators have given meaning to that general phrase. There would be no greater difficulty in applying the same technique to disciplinary action by a union against its members.

Since discipline less serious than expulsion or deprivation of voting rights does not take away a man's right to take part in collective bargaining by participating in union affairs, there is no justification for outside review of such penalties as a fine. However, if a fine is imposed and the member is thereafter expelled for failure to pay the fine, the entire course of events should be open to review.

Any new legislation should grant every employee in an established bargaining unit a right to membership and full voting rights in the union that acts as the bargaining representative unless he has engaged in conduct which would justify his expulsion under the standards described above. The reasons for creating a legal right to union membership have been stated. It should be observed, however, that my suggestion applies only to employees who are already employed in the bargaining unit. It is the fact of employment in the bargaining unit which creates the need of a right to membership. Under the Taft-Hartley Act, union membership is not a condition of obtaining employment. Employers and unions are forbidden to discriminate among applicants for employment by reason of membership or nonmembership in a labor organization.[54] So long as these provisions are part of our existing labor law there would seem to be no need to consider federal legislation dealing with a right to membership before employment in the bargaining unit.

Were such a statute to be enacted it might provide alternate

---

[54] NLRA 8 (a)(3), 8 (b)(2).

methods of enforcement. Where the government must do the job, the administration of the statute could be vested in the National Labor Relations Board. The familiar unfair labor-practice procedure is well adapted to the need. But I would like to see the unions encouraged to establish their own independent appeal boards along the lines initiated by the Upholsterers International Union and followed by the United Automobile Workers. This could be done by authorizing the secretary of labor to issue periodic certificates exempting a union from enforcement proceedings instituted by the NLRB upon finding that the union had established an independent appeal board where a union member or applicant for membership would receive at least as great protection as before the NLRB.

This procedure would bring the cases much closer to the people affected. It would preserve a larger measure of informality, flexibility, and self-government. It would minimize government intervention in internal union affairs.

Under either procedure outside review should not be available until there has been a fair opportunity for the labor organization and any parent body to review the case and correct any mistake or injustice. The principal problem is to allow enough time for self-government without permitting delay. The executive boards of many international unions meet quarterly. Appeal to a convention is unduly time-consuming. Perhaps it would strike a fair balance to allow an expelled member to invoke the processes of the NLRB or independent appeal boards only if he can show *that he has exhausted the remedies reasonably available to him under the constitution and bylaws of the labor organization, including any right of appeal, or has invoked such remedies without obtaining a final decision within six months of his resort thereto.*

One more word seems appropriate. Section 8 (a) (3) of the NLRA permits the execution of union-shop contracts but forbids an employer to discriminate against an employee who lost his union membership for any reason other than nonpayment of dues. This limitation was put into the Taft-Hartley Act in order to prevent a union from using control over its members' jobs for such purposes as punishing the exercise of free speech, engaging in political activities distasteful to the union, testifying against the union, and refusing to engage in slowdowns. The restriction goes beyond the evil. It denies a union the power to use the union shop as a means of disciplining those who engaged in plainly improper conduct such as leading a wildcat strike, engaging in espionage against the union, or otherwise aiding the employer. Any legislation providing for the review of all expulsions and denials of membership, would give adequate protection against the abuse of disciplinary power. The final proviso to Section 8 (a) (3) could then be repealed.

ELECTIONS

The election of union officers is the heart of the democratic process. The policies of a large organization must be formulated and administered by a smaller group of officials. Their responsiveness to the members depends upon the frequence of elections, a fair opportunity to nominate and vote for candidates, and an honest count of the ballots.

Present Law.—The law has developed few legal principles concerning the conduct of labor-union elections. The member who complains that an election has not been held or that the nominations or voting were not conducted in accordance with the constitution and bylaws cannot maintain an action for damages because he has sustained no measurable loss. The remedy, if any, must be a decree ousting the officers or ordering an election. This kind of injunctive relief is available only in a court of equity, and here the complaining members are likely to find the threshold barred by the old rule that equity acts only for the protection of property.[55] In *Leahigh v. Beyer*,[56] for example, the court refused to interfere with an allegedly improper run-off election in a UAW local union because "no individual property rights of any of the plaintiffs are in any manner affected or involved in the action of defendants sought to be relieved against." [57]

In some jurisdictions there is greater hope of relief. Some courts have found the property interest necessary to give jurisdiction in the risk of misappropriation of union funds and have gone on to supervise the conduct of an election as an incident to the protection of the assets.[58] Others have given lip service to the rule that equity intervenes only for the protection of property by saying that the right to elect union officers is as much a right of property as the right to union membership. In *Raevsky v. Upholsterers' International Union of North America* [59] the court retained jurisdiction of a bill to enjoin the international president from interfering with an election saying:

It may well be here that the officers have the authority to distribute jobs, collect dues, make expenditures, control the property of the union, pay out strike benefits, and represent the union with the employer. These we know are typical of trade-union duties, through their agents. These are important powers, which in the hands of leaders seeking economic or personal gain may be abused to the detriment of members of a trade union. Such an abuse of power might interfere with the economic welfare of the members as much as expulsion from the union itself. Moreover, it can be said that the right to have an election within a trade union is a property right

---

[55] E.g. *Stanton v. Harris*, 152 Fla. 736, 13 So.2d 17 (1943); State ex rel. *Givens v. Superior Court*, 233 Ind. 235, 117 N.E.2d 553 (1954). See also *Finley v. Duffy*, 154 Ohio St. 390, 94 N.E.2d 465 (1950); *Way v. Patton*, 195 Ore. 36, 241 P.2d 895 (1952).

[56] 116 N.E.2d 458 (Oh. C.P. 1953).

[57] *Ibid.* at 462.

[58] E.g. *Wilson v. Miller*, 194 Tenn. 390, 250 S.W.2d 575 (1952).

[59] 38 Pa. D. & C. 187 (1940).

which courts have recognized: See 86 U. of Pa. Law Rev. 885, and cases there cited.

The cases cited in defendants' brief are for the most part distinguishable because they concern political associations in which the court was unable to find a property right which had been abrogated. Social clubs, political clubs and trade unions, though all with the same basis of unincorporation, must be differentiated. Our modern economic life so dictates.[60]

The Pennsylvania [61] and New Jersey [62] courts have intervened in union elections without considering the basis of jurisdiction.[63]

Perhaps the law will adopt the more liberal view. Dean Pound demonstrated forty years ago that equity often intervenes to protect interests of personality.[64] The underlying reason for denying jurisdiction must have been reluctance to intervene in the internal affairs of associations which the judges regarded as no less voluntary than a social club. The current power of unions and the community's new concern for democratic control may soon be reflected in freer intervention in states where the issue is not foreclosed by precedent—and these are by far the greatest number.

But even if the threshold is passed, the courts are not likely to be useful instruments for ensuring democratic union elections. Three obstacles stand in the way.

1) A court can do no more than enforce the union's own

[60] *Ibid.* at 195.
[61] *O'Neil v. United Association of Journeymen Plumbers and Steamfitters*, 348 Pa. 531, 36 A.2d 325 (1944); *Maloney v. United Mine Workers of America*, 308 Pa. 251, 161 A.2d 538 (1932); See *O'Hara v. Teamsters, Chauffeurs, Warehousemen and Helpers*, 36 Pa. D. & C. 573 (1948).
[62] *Sibilia v. Western Electric Employees Association*, 142 N.J. Eq. 77, 59 A.2d 251 (1948).
[63] See also *O'Connell v. O'Leary*, 167 Misc. 324, 3 N.Y.S.2d 833 (Sup. Ct. 1938); *Dusing v. Nuzzo*, 177 Misc. 35, 29 N.Y.S.2d 882 (Sup. Ct. 1941), modified and affirmed 263 App. Div. 59 (3d Dept. 1941). In some situations the claim to the salary for an office may give the losing candidate a right to sue.
[64] Pound, *op. cit.* (n. 12).

constitution and bylaws. By stretching a point perhaps a court could also invalidate any constitutional provision which was contrary to public policy, but even this would do little to enforce democratic control. The court cannot provide a substitute for the provision which it invalidates. It cannot write a union constitution. It cannot prescribe the time, place, and frequency of elections, create machinery for nominations or define the electorate. In short, without the aid of legislation, the common law cannot supply minimum electoral guarantees if they are missing from the union constitution.

2) A court is also a clumsy instrument for supervising an election. The judicial process may be well enough adapted to trying the validity of an election that has already been held; but if it is found invalid, or if no election has been held, judges have few facilities for providing an effective remedy. Merely to order an election might turn the authority to conduct the balloting over to the very same officers whose misconduct gave rise to the litigation. The court has no tellers, watchers, or similar officials. It would become mired in the details of the electoral process. To appoint a master to supervise the election would delegate the responsibility, but the master would face many of the same problems as the judge. Probably it is the consciousness of these weaknesses that has made judges so reluctant to interfere with union elections, but apparently a few court-conducted elections have been held.[65]

3) The normal rules concerning the exhaustion of administrative remedies would often postpone judicial action until it was too late. Perhaps other judges would be less strict than the judge who dismissed the plaintiff's case for failure to exhaust his administrative remedies even though the plaintiff showed that the contested term of office would expire while

---

[65] *Dusing v. Nuzzo,* 177 Misc. 35, 29 N.Y.S.2d 882 (Sup. Ct. 1941), modified and affirmed 263 App. Div. 59 (3d Dept. 1941). *O'Neil v. United Association of Journeymen Plumbers and Steamfitters,* 348 Pa. 531, 36 A.2d 325 (1944); *Wilson v. Miller,* 194 Tenn. 390, 250 S.W.2d 575.

the appeal was being processed,[66] but there is scant indication that they would insist on the necessary speed.

By suggesting the inability of the common law to guarantee democratic union elections I do not mean to imply that new law is required. The existence of abuses has not been factually demonstrated. Apparently there were widespread violations of the constitution and bylaws of the International Brotherhood of Teamsters in the choice of delegates for the 1957 convention but many of them were technical and no one seriously believes that a majority of the members desired a different president. In other internationals union receiverships may have affected the choice of convention delegates.[67] A few unions elect officers for excessive terms. Apart from these specific problems, however, I know of no factual basis for doubting the integrity of union elections.

Of course the argument for basic guarantees does not necessarily rest on proof of actual wrongdoing. If unions are designed to serve the democratic purposes of the community and if the law gives them the special statutory power necessary to fulfill these functions, then perhaps the community should provide such electoral guarantees as may be necessary to achieve the ultimate objectives and keep the statutory power from being abused. Furthermore, it may not be enough that union elections are actually fair. Like Caesar's wife—and for the same reasons—union elections must be above both justified and unjustified suspicion. Here again I suggest that the problem boils down to a question of balance. If guarantees can be devised which would not impair the independence, strength, or orderly functioning of labor unions, their enactment would minimize the risk of autocratic control. On the other hand,

---

[66] *Leahigh v. Beyer,* 116 N.E.2d 458 (Oh. C.P. 1953).

[67] The McClellan Committee found that 13 per cent of the Teamsters locals were in receivership and twelve locals carried 20 per cent of the membership of the International Union of Operating Engineers. In some internationals the receivers name the convention delegates who would therefore be amenable to the directions of the international officers,

if such a law would carry inevitable costs, its enactment should
be delayed pending more careful investigation of the practical necessity.

Proposed Legislation.—During the past year there has been
much talk about the need for federal legislation guaranteeing
fair and democratic union elections. The administration has
introduced one proposal.[68] The McClellan Committee recom-
mends action but supplied no specifications.[69] Senators Knowl-
and,[70] Ives,[71] and McClellan [72] have introduced different bills.

The administration bill offers a curiously complicated, back-
handed arrangement. Section 102 requires every labor organization to file detailed financial statements, elaborate reports
concerning its internal procedures, and also a certificate that

the organization holds elections at intervals not less often than
once every four years in which all members of the labor organization in good standing are entitled to and are accorded the opportunity to participate, upon due notice, in the election of their
local officers directly by secret vote of the members or through
representatives to delegate bodies who are elected directly by
secret vote of the members.

Section 303 authorizes the secretary to investigate the truth
of the certificate and to hold administrative hearings to determine whether there was a willful failure to file a true report. If
the secretary finds a violation, he may deny the union the
right to institute proceedings before the National Labor Relations Board and may also revoke its exemption from income
taxes for a period not exceeding five years.

The administration bill would have two obvious consequences. First, it would compel some unions to amend their
constitutions so as to elect their officers every four years instead of at longer intervals. The four-year limit is also fixed

---

[68] S.3097, 85 Cong. 2d sess.
[69] S.Rep. 1417, 85th Cong. 2d sess. 452 (1958).
[70] S.3068, 85 Cong. 2d sess.
[71] Irving Ives, Press Release, November 21, 1957.
[72] S.3618, 85 Cong. 2d sess.

by Code VI of the AFL-CIO Ethical Practices Committee. Second, the bill would require the election of delegates and local officers by secret ballot. The wisdom of the latter provision may be debatable. Many local unions now choose their officers in an open vote, and it is sometimes argued that this prevents a dishonest count of the ballots. The risk is obvious but on the whole I am inclined to believe that the balance is in favor of secret elections. The chance of a dishonest count may be increased, but the risks of packing the hall or of intimidation and reprisal are greatly diminished.

It is not clear whether the administration bill does more than impose these two formal constitutional requirements. Would the certificate mean that all members were *in fact* accorded the opportunity to vote or only that the constitution so specifies? Would the certificate imply that there was an honest count of the ballots so that the secretary might look into charges attacking the integrity of the process? And the opportunity to nominate candidates, a matter upon which the bill is silent, seems no less important than the opportunity to vote.

There are strong grounds for criticizing the machinery established by the bill. If it is a proper function of government to require regular union elections by secret ballot, the government should lay down the rules and punish violations instead of requiring the filing of a certificate, then investigating whether the certificate was "willfully" false, and finally depriving the union of its income-tax exemptions and standing before the National Labor Relations Board. The more direct approach would have the following advantages: it would permit a simple statement of rules which union officials could learn and follow; it would permit direct investigation of alleged violations, prompt action to set aside an invalid election, and the supervision of a new vote; and it would eliminate the improper sanctions proposed by the administration. The rights and duties created by the National Labor Relations Act exist for the benefit of the public. Such legal obligations should be enforced equally in all cases, not traded off against one another as a system of rewards and punishments. Furthermore, any union officers who willfully fail to file the reports are the wrongdoers. The proposed sanction would unfairly put the burden of the punishment upon the union members whom it is the very purpose of the legislation to protect.

It is still more foolish to use a labor union's exemption from income tax as a sanction. The financial penalties would often be disproportionate to the offense. The enforcement agency would be compelled to choose between imposing an excessive penalty and overlooking the violation. To create such dilemmas makes for unsound law enforcement. Again, the purpose of the legislation is to protect union members. A failure to conduct democratic elections is essentially a wrong done by the officers against the members. To deny the union the usual income-tax exemption would hardly punish the officers. It would levy a heavy penalty upon the members who are the ultimate owners of the union's property, who benefit from its availability, and who have committed no offense.

Senator Knowland's bill (S.3068) goes far beyond the administration's proposal. It requires the quadrennial election of officers by a secret popular vote. International officers would have to be chosen by a referendum instead of a convention. Also, upon petition of 15 per cent of the members the National Labor Relations Board is directed to conduct a secret ballot as often as once a year upon the recall of any officer. Upon like petition the board must also conduct a referendum upon almost any question pertaining to union business. Upon petition of 15 per cent of the employees in the bargaining unit the board must conduct a vote upon whether to call or continue a strike.

Time forbids marshaling all the grounds for criticizing the Knowland bill. The fundamental objection is that it turns over to an arm of the state the responsibility of carrying on the internal governmental processes of a labor union without any showing that the union officers and members were incompetent or corrupt. Such a measure does not promote freedom or democracy. It reduces self-government. It denies the private responsibility and self-determination which lie at the heart of a voluntary association. The same objection applies to the election provisions of Senator McClellan's bill.[73]

Another objection is that popular elections, popular recall, and the formulation of policy by referendum are neither efficient nor truly democratic ways of conducting union business. A small minority could keep the organization in a constant state of turmoil. It would tie up union affairs by demanding an NLRB vote upon any program which it opposed. Secret popular balloting among the members of a national or international union would simply add to the difficulty of ousting "the administration." At a convention the opposition need only persuade an informed group of delegates whereas in a referendum it must build up national popularity in competition with the only names well known to all the members; and the incumbents control the union newspaper which is the chief vehicle for communication with the members. Similarly, a secret yes or no vote on an issue of union policy withholds the opportunities to influence the outcome which are present at a meeting where there can be discussion, compromise, and adjustment.

The fallacies of strike votes have been discussed too often for further comment.

If we assume the desirability of legislation guaranteeing the democratic election of union officials, the soundest approach may lie somewhere between the administration and Knowland bills. It should require the election of union "officers"[74] every four years either by secret ballot or in a convention.[75]

---

[73] S.3618, 85 Cong. 2d sess.

[74] The term "officers" denotes the class of officers required to file non-Communist affidavits under NLRA A 9(h) and the NLRB regulations.

[75] A referendum by mail would be an acceptable form of secret ballot.

If the election is by convention, the delegates must be chosen by secret ballot. The requirement of quadrennial elections should apply to both international and local unions.

An election every four years will prevent the establishment of an entrenched autocracy. Many unions, especially local unions, hold more frequent elections but this should be a matter of choice. Too frequent elections may keep a union unstable. They tend to discourage sound and courageous leadership. Candidates for union office are usually under pressure to take aggressive positions and to prosecute every grievance or demand, however far-fetched, in the hope of winning support for their candidacy. A reasonable term in office enables an official to devote himself to building constructive collective bargaining relationships.

The statute should establish other requirements: Members should be given due notice of the time and place of an election; there should be a reasonable opportunity to nominate candidates; all members in good standing should be permitted to vote without coercion or restraint—thus the law should forbid intimidation of voters, denials of the right to vote, and dishonest counting of the ballots; all records pertaining to the election would have to be preserved to enable higher union officials and the government to investigate charges of dishonesty.

No honest and democratic labor union would have any difficulty in meeting these elementary requirements. The responsibility for carrying them out should therefore be left to the regular union officials until a shortcoming is proved. Similarly, the unions should be left free to work out the details concerning eligibility to run for office, the time and place of the election, the manner of nominating candidates, the manner of voting (*e.g.*, by mail or at a polling place), and the like. In these areas the government need do no more than impose the duty to comply with the union's own constitution and bylaws.

It would be unsound to adopt Senator Ives' proposal for requiring a secret ballot on all issues that arise in the normal conduct of union affairs.[76] Such a law, if strictly enforced, would tie up the conduct of union business and lead to long dull meetings, which fewer and fewer members would attend. If loosely written, such a law could be evaded by amending the constitution and bylaws to delegate greater authority to the officers or executive board. In either event there would be a lessening of true democracy rather than an increase.

The ultimate responsibility for enforcement might be vested in the National Labor Relations Board. The right to file charges should be limited to members, and any member challenging an election on the ground that the statute had been violated should be required first to pursue his remedies within the labor union and any parent body. This rule would preserve a maximum of independence and self-government by giving every labor organization an opportunity to correct improper local elections. If the member is denied relief or can obtain no decision from the union one way or the other within three months, he should be allowed to file a charge with the National Labor Relations Board. Since time is important, no charge should be entertained more than four months after an election. If the union's own review procedure took more than four months, the member would have to elect between his internal and statutory remedies.

Upon receipt of a proper charge the NLRB should make an investigation in order to ascertain whether there is reasonable cause to believe that the law has been violated. If it found reasonable cause, it would institute and prosecute formal proceedings against the labor organization in a manner analogous to the familiar unfair labor-practice proceedings.

If the NLRB should decide that there had been no election within four years or that a substantial violation of the statute or the constitution and bylaws of the organization might have

---

[76] Irving Ives, Press Release, November 21, 1957.

affected the outcome of an election, it would direct a new election to be held under its supervision. After the election it would certify the names of the persons elected who would thereupon become the officers of the labor organization.

There should also be provision for judicial enforcement and review of an order certifying the results of an election conducted by the NLRB. The power of the court would reach back to the decision on the validity of the original election but no other decision or orders should be subject to appeal.

I would also suggest that state legislation should be inapplicable to labor organizations covered by the federal law and that court litigation should be precluded. This important provision seems justified by the following considerations:

There is need for uniformity. International and national unions operate in many states. It would be confusing, unduly burdensome, and often impossible for them to comply with a variety of election laws. No corporation is subject to such burdens in the election of its officers.

The same considerations apply with lesser force to local unions. A considerable number function in several states. Also, the burden of checking compliance is likely to fall upon the international union. It is easier to enforce one uniform rule than a crazy quilt of state legislation.

Ill-considered state laws would interfere with the national labor policy. Too stringent laws would handicap unions in dealing with employers. Too frequent elections may keep a local union in a state of restlessness. A comparatively stable leadership can devote itself to constructive action thereby serving both employees and the public.

One more point is significant. Since union business must not be brought to a standstill whenever an election is challenged, it would be necessary to make some provision for the conduct of business while the proceeding is in progress. It would be intolerable for the government to appoint outsiders to act as receivers. The choice lies between keeping the old officers in office or allowing the new officers to enter upon their duties even though their right may be challenged. The latter course seems preferable for several reasons. A union election should be presumed valid until the contrary appears. The newly elected officers are those most likely to have the support of the members. There would be the least disruption of normal procedure within the union. However, the ultimate decisions upon this point should be made by the labor unions themselves. Consequently any bill should provide that pending final action by the National Labor Relations Board the election should be presumed valid and the affairs of the union should be administered by the new officers or in such other manner as the constitution and bylaws might provide.

TRUSTEESHIPS AND RECEIVERSHIPS

The constitutions of many international unions authorize the international officers to suspend the normal government of a constituent local union, assume control of its property, and conduct its affairs. Under some constitutions charges must be filed against the local and a hearing must be held before the international intervenes. Under others, the general president can take over a local without a hearing, subject to approval of the General Executive Board after a hearing. Apparently there are still a few international unions which make no provision for a hearing. The guiding standard is usually very vague. For example, the constitution of the Hotel and Restaurant Employees provides that the general president may appoint a trustee whenever the local has conducted its affairs "contrary to the interests of such local or the international union, so as to constitute a threat to the welfare of such organizations, or in a grossly incompetent manner, or where an emergency exists." [77] Although the device has various

---

[77] *Mixed Local of Hotel and Restaurant Employees v. Hotel and Restaurant Employees International Alliance*, 212 Minn. 587, 4 N.W.2d 771 (1942).

names, I shall use the term "trusteeship" loosely to describe any form of supervision by which an international union takes over the affairs of a subordinate unit.

It needs no argument to demonstrate that placing a local union in trusteeship constitutes a serious impairment of both liberty and self-government. Thereafter all decisions affecting the local are made by officials appointed by the international. The local officers are suspended. There are no new local elections. The members can hold no meetings unless the trustee approves. Often the members lose even the power to choose delegates to international conventions, thus becoming unable to influence the policies of the international or the conduct of its affairs. It seems probable, moreover, that the threat of imposing trusteeship is often an effective way of compelling a local union to conform to the instructions of the international officers contrary to the original desire of the members.

Nevertheless, any thoughtful discussion of union trusteeships must recognize their indispensability. Trusteeships are one device, perhaps the primary device, by which international officers can keep the labor movement strong and effective, untainted by corruption, and free from subversion. In his testimony before the Labor Subcommittee of the Senate Committee on Labor and Public Welfare AFL-CIO President Meany accurately described some of the problems which justify the appointment of trustees.[78] He said:

A trusteeship may be necessary to bring about the honest administration of local union funds. "Dishonest persons occasionally secure local union office and embezzle or misuse the funds of the local union. Sometimes local union officers are extravagant or improvident and involve a local union in financial difficulties without their being actually dishonest. Sometimes local union officers refuse to follow the standards laid

[78] The excerpts are quoted from pp. 15–17 of the mimeographed statement filed with the subcommittee.

down by the international for the maintenance of proper financial books and records, so that it is impossible for auditors of the international union to ascertain whether or not financial practices are being engaged in. In any of these situations the international may deem it necessary to establish a trusteeship."

A trusteeship may be an essential step to the restoration of freedom and democracy within a local union. "Occasionally a local union officer or business agent secures complete control of the local, and becomes a virtual dictator. He may fail to call membership meetings, hold no elections and simply run the union to suit himself."

A trusteeship may be the means of freeing a subordinate body from racketeers or Communist control.

Mr. Meany might have added at least two other situations to his list:

Occasionally local officers act irresponsibly in collective bargaining or lose control over the members. The calling of unauthorized strikes in violation of the international's constitution or the inability or unwillingness to honor collective-bargaining commitments is a proper cause for international intervention.[79]

Besides, if a union becomes so torn by dissent that its business is demoralized, or if local officers and members become too lazy to service existing contracts or organize nonunion firms, the suspension of local autonomy may be the only way to rebuild an effective local organization.

Unfortunately trusteeships have also been a virulent source of political autocracy and financial corruption. Some of the most notorious are familiar to every student of labor history. Thousands of dollars were extracted from laborers and contractors in the building of the Delaware River Aqueduct through the activities of Bove, Nuzzo, and their associates with

---

[79] *Cromwell v. Morrin*, 91 N.Y.S.2d 176 (Sup. Ct. 1949).

the connivance, if not support, of the international officers of the Hod Carriers Union.[80] The autocratic direction of the United Mine Workers results at least in part from the suspension of local self-government. Twelve local unions of the International Union of Operating Engineers representing 20 per cent of the membership are held under international supervision. Seven have been in trusteeship for at least ten years; two for twenty-nine years.[81] The McClellan Committee also found that 13 per cent of all locals in the International Brotherhood of Teamsters are under trusteeships; some of them were taken over more than fifteen years before.[82] No one should suppose that these faults are characteristic of the labor movement but they are nevertheless cause for great public concern.

There appear to be these chief motivations for the imposition of improper trusteeships:

First, the opportunity to loot rich local treasuries has been a significant temptation.[83]

Second, the desire to control the policies of a local union may stem from honorable motives but frequently has been evidence of a desire to use union position for personal advantage.[84]

Third, other trusteeships have been imposed in order to keep in office men friendly to the international union. The McClellan Committee reports that when a Teamsters local in Pontiac, Michigan, revolted against four officials who had

[80] See *Dusing v. Nuzzo*, 177 Misc. 35, 29 N.Y.S.2d 882 (Sup. Ct. 1941), modified and affirmed 263 App. Div. 59 (3rd Dept. 1941); *Moore v. Moreschi*, 179 Misc. 475, 39 N.Y. Supp. 207 (Sup. Ct. 1942), affirmed 265 App. Div. 989 (1st. Dept. 1943), modified and affirmed 291 N.Y. 81 (1943); *Canfield v. Moreschi*, 268 App. Div. 64, 48 N.Y.S.2d 668 (3d Dept. 1944), affirmed 294 N.Y. 632, 64 N.E.2d 177 (1945).

[81] S. Rep. 1417, 85th Cong. 2d sess. 371.

[82] *Ibid.* at 448.

[83] See cases cited n. 77.

[84] This statement is based on a number of trusteeships described in the McClellan Committee hearings.

been accused of extortion, the international put the local under the trusteeship of James Hoffa who then appointed two of the four officials as business agents to run the affairs of the local.[85]

Finally, the imposition of a trusteeship may be a method of controlling an international convention. Frequently the trustee appoints the delegates of the local union under his control. Since the general president will name a trustee friendly to himself, the trustee may be expected to follow the president's suggestions in choosing delegates, and the delegates themselves will not be blind to their dependence upon the president's good will. With 10 or 20 per cent of the membership in trusteeships the international officers would have a strong bloc of votes.

Present Law.—There is little indication that the courts afford local union members adequate protection against abuse of the trusteeship device. The law approaches the problem in much the same way as the discipline of union members. Equity will intervene in the affairs of a voluntary association in order to protect property rights. Just as the interest of an individual in the assets of a union is threatened by improper expulsion, so the combined interests of the members of a local are threatened by the suspension of the local or the deprivation of its charter.[86] Most of the cases expressly decide or silently assume that the appointment of trustees or institution of international supervision has a like effect upon the property rights of the local members.[87]

In exercising this jurisdiction the courts are governed chiefly by implications of the doctrine that the constitution and by-laws of a voluntary association are a contract between the

---

[85] S.Rep. 1417, 85th Cong. 2d sess. 448.

[86] *Supreme Lodge of the World Loyal Order of Moose v. Los Angeles Lodge No. 386*, 177 Cal. 132, 169 Pac. 1040 (1917); *Neal v. Hutcheson*, 160 N.Y. Supp. 1007 (1916).

[87] For example, *Robinson v. Nick*, 235 Mo. App. 461, 136 S.W.2d 374 (1940). See also cases cited in notes 85–86.

association and the members. Trustees designated by an international union will be enjoined from interfering with the property of a local if the international officers fail to follow constitutional procedures.[88] Furthermore the rule seems to be settled, again by analogy to cases dealing with the discipline of individual members, that receivers may not be appointed to take over a local unless there is a fair hearing including notice of the charges and an opportunity to present a defense.[89] The rule is one imposed by law in the sense that the court will read it into ambiguous constitutions and even disregard any constitutional provision which authorizes a receivership without a hearing.[90]

There is some doubt whether the hearing must precede the trusteeship. Several cases upheld constitutional provisions authorizing the general president to appoint trustees subject to an appeal before the general executive board in which the local union can be heard within thirty days of the trustee's appointment.[91] A minority rule apparently requires an earlier hearing on the ground that it is unfair to put the members of the local under the burden of upsetting a determination which has already been made.[92] The former rule seems preferable.

---

[88] *Canfield v. Moreschi,* 268 App. Div. 64, 48 N.Y.S.2d 668 (3d Dept. 1944), affirmed 294 N.Y. 632, 64 N.E.2d 177 (1945).

[89] See *Local 373, International Association of Bridge Ironworkers v. International Association of Bridge Ironworkers,* 120 N.J. Eq. 220, 230, 184 Atl. 531, 535 (Ct. Err. & App. 1936); *Neal v. Hutcheson,* 160 N.Y. Supp. 1007, 1010 (Sup. Ct. 1916).

[90] *Washington Local Lodge No. 194 v. International Brotherhood of Boilermakers,* 33 Wn.2d 1, 203 P.2d 1019 (1949); *Local No. 373 v. International Association of Iron Workers,* 120 N.J. Eq. 220, 184 A.531, *Neal v. Hutcheson,* 160 N.Y. Supp. 1007 (Sup. Ct. 1916). See *Garcia v. Ernst,* 101 N.Y.S.2d 693 (Sup. Ct. 1950).

[91] *Mixed Local of Hotel and Restaurant Employees v. Hotel and Restaurant Employees International Alliance,* 212 Minn. 587, 4 N.W.2d 771 (1942); *Garcia v. Ernst,* 27 L.R.R.M. 2497 (N.Y. Sup. Ct. 1951); *Fanara v. International Brotherhood of Teamsters,* 34 L.R.R.M. 2714 (N.Y. Sup. Ct. 1954).

[92] *Kennedy v. Schroeder,* 35 N.Y.S.2d 835 (Sup. Ct. 1942) reversed on other grounds 265 App. Div. 725, 40 N.Y.S.2d 611; *Reiser v. Kralstein,* 26 L.R.R.M. 2264 (N.Y. Sup. Ct. 1950).

For example, if the local officers are engaged in financial chicanery, the assets of the local can be protected only by swift intervention. The burden of upsetting the earlier determination would not be excessive if the hearing were conducted before a body that had not already passed upon the question; indeed a proceeding before the same body would not be a fair hearing within the meaning of the rule.[93]

There are few reported decisions staying or upsetting trusteeships on substantive grounds. Under the contract theory the essential question is whether the constitution has been violated. The vagueness of most constitutional provisions regarding receiverships is exceeded only by their breadth. In one case the judge was satisfied that the International Association of Machinists had instituted international supervision in order to suppress criticism of the president's misconduct.[94] In the Delaware River Aqueduct cases the lower courts found that the International intervened in bad faith, apparently meaning that the ostensible justification was only a pretense to conceal intended racketeering, but the court of appeals rather carefully based its affirmance upon the want of fair hearing before the trusteeships were imposed.[95]

There is also pragmatic evidence of the inability of the common law to grant local union members adequate protection against unjust trusteeships. Thirteen per cent of the Teamsters locals are in trusteeships; some of them have lasted fifteen years. Recently Hoffa was trustee of seventeen different locals. Twenty per cent of the members of the Operating Engineers belong to locals in trusteeship; nine of them have lasted more than ten years. Perhaps these facts evi-

---

[93] *Spitzer v. Ernst*, 20 L.R.R.M. 2487 (N.Y. Sup. Ct. 1947).

[94] The determination was made on motion for a temporary injunction. *Schrank v. Brown*, 192 Misc. 80, 80 N.Y. Supp. 452 (Sup. Ct. 1948). In later proceedings this issue dropped out of the case. See 194 Misc. 138, 86 N.Y.S.2d 209 (1949).

[95] *Moore v. Moreschi*, 179 Misc. 475, affirmed 265 App. Div. 989, modified and affirmed 291 N.Y. 81 (1943).

dence only an indifference to self-government so long as the
union officialdom proves reasonably efficient in securing
higher wages for the members, but I am inclined to think
that the more likely explanation lies in the practical impedi-
ments to using what little theoretical protection the common
law affords.

1) The cost of legal proceedings is likely to be heavy.
The individual members have little property with which to
pay lawyers' fees, post bonds, and print voluminous records.
If the suit is successful the court may allow fees out of the
union's funds. If the suit fails, the individuals bear the
cost.

2) Even if the suit is successful, the individual members
will reap no monetary advantage. Occasionally a group of
members may feel strongly enough to institute an action in
order to protect what they feel are intangible rights, but
most men would not regard this as a sufficient inducement
for risking financial loss.

3) Time is on the side of the defendants. The doctrine of
exhaustion of remedies opens the way to dilatory appeals.

4) The individual member who institutes an action against
international officers runs enormous risks, and the more arbitrary the imposition of the trusteeship the greater are the risks
imposed. Many union constitutions forbid a member to bring
an action against the union without exhausting his internal
remedies. Workers have been subjected to fines as large as
$1,000 for bringing such suits; others have been expelled
from the union.[96] The law concerning exhaustion of remedies
is far too flexible for a lawyer safely to predict when they
have been exhausted, nor can one be sure just how the union
officials named as defendants will interpret the constitutional
provision. Other constitutions provide for expulsion for in-
stituting any action against the union. It seeems unlikely
that many members are aware of their invalidity and even if

---

[96] Summers, 64 *Harv. L. Rev.* pp. 1067–1068.

the members knew the law, it is unlikely that they would choose to take the risk. In many industries expulsion from a union means loss of employment, the Taft-Hartley Act to the contrary notwithstanding, and there are other ways by which entrenched officials can "take care of" the recalcitrant. With all these risks added to the financial burden, it takes a brave and stubborn man to challenge a trusteeship.

Proposed Legislation.—International trusteeships are one of the favorite targets of labor bills, and one of the most difficult to hit in the bull's-eye. The McClellan Committee report makes a general recommendation for some "restriction on the baseless imposition of trusteeships and supervisorships for periods as long as 30 years." [97] Senator Knowland's bill would impose three requirements enforceable by a private suit for an injunction in the federal district court: A trusteeship should not be imposed except in conformity with the constitution and bylaws of the labor organization; during the receivership the funds of the local union, except the normal per capita tax, should be used exclusively in connection with the affairs of the local organization; and no trusteeship should last more than one year. [98]

Senator McClellan's bill would compel every union to insert into its constitution a clause limiting the duration of a trusteeship to one year unless the membership of the local union should be willing to continue it for another year in a referendum by secret ballot. [99] The bill apparently imposes no other limitations upon trusteeships.

Senator Kennedy has also introduced a bill intended to curtail the abuses of trusteeships which was drafted after careful study by a group of professional advisors. Section 201 sets up two standards for testing the legality of a trusteeship:

[97] S.Rep. 1417, 85th Cong. 2d sess. 452.
[98] S.3068, 85th Cong. 2d sess.
[99] S.3618, 85th Cong. 2d sess.

The trusteeship must conform to the constitution and by-laws of the labor organization.

The trusteeship must be imposed for one of the following purposes: "correcting corruption or financial malpractice, assuring the performance of collective bargaining agreements or other duties of a bargaining representative, or otherwise carrying out the legitimate objects [of the international union]."

These standards are somewhat general, especially the last, but we are in an area where it is very difficult to find abstract criteria for separating measures essential to strong internal government from subterfuges which are oppressive or corrupt. On the other hand, it should not be a difficult decision to make in a particular case after the facts were developed—certainly no more difficult than deciding what is an unreasonable restraint of trade or an unfair method of competition. Section 203 vests enforcement in the National Labor Relations Board, subject to an important qualification, so that through the usual administrative process the agency may build up criteria for applying the general statutory standard to concrete situations. The NLRB proceedings would be conducted in the same manner as unfair labor-practice cases.

The Kennedy bill also supplies the NLRB with one firm guide line for determining whether a receivership meets the statutory standard. Recognizing the delicate judgments which international officers are called upon to make in imposing a trusteeship and conscious of the relative inexpertness of outsiders, it is provided that for the first year a trusteeship "shall be presumed valid . . . and shall not be subject to attack except upon proof that the trusteeship was not established in good faith for a purpose allowable under section 201." [100]

The presumption is available, however, only if the trusteeship was instituted in procedural conformity with the con-

[100] S.3454, 85th Cong. 2d sess., section 203 (c).

stitution and bylaws of the international labor organization and "authorized or ratified by its general executive board after a fair hearing." The language adopts the view that the rush of events may force the international president to act without a hearing and therefore permits the hearing to be held after the trustee has been appointed. The desire to gain the benefit of the presumption should be enough to induce a union to allow a hearing at one time or another.[101]

The presumption seems justifiable because the obnoxious element of trusteeships is not their imposition but their duration. The initial suspension of local self-government is usually justified by the needs of the organization, and it would unreasonably impair the independence of the labor movement to allow much scope at this point for the government to review the judgment of union officials upon the needs of the organization or the best means of effectuating them. On the other hand, the local emergency that justifies international intervention can normally be resolved in a relatively short period. There is a superficial temptation therefore to fix a rigid statutory limit for duration of trusteeships such as the one-year period proposed in the Knowland bill. Upon more careful analysis, however, the dangers of any arbitrary time limit seem clear. If Communists capture a local union, it may be more than a year before the international officers can build up a group of loyal trade unionists able and willing to govern their own affairs despite skilled subversion. Unhappily the entire leadership of a local may be corrupt and its ouster leaves a vacuum which is not easily filled. For such reasons, I suggest that although we can fix a rule of thumb of the outer limit beyond which a trusteeship usually ought not to last there must nevertheless be some provision for flexibility.

The Kennedy bill solves this problem by reversing the

---

[101] The provision for ratification is included because a general president must sometimes move very rapidly in order to halt financial mismanagement or corruption.

presumption which applies during the first year. Section
203 (c) provides:

> After the expiration of one year such a trusteeship shall be pre-
> sumed invalid unless the labor organization concerned shall show
> by clear and convincing proof that the continuation of the trustee-
> ship is necessary for a purpose allowable under section 201.[102]

If a trusteeship is needed for more than one year, surely the
international officers ought to be able to demonstrate the
reason.

The Kennedy bill also deals with two specific abuses often
incident to trusteeships. Section 202 makes it a crime to transfer to the international union any funds of the local except the
normal per capita tax and assessments payable by subordinate bodies not in trusteeship. This provision would prevent
the appointment of trustees for the purpose of "milking" a
local treasury. The same section makes it unlawful to count
the votes of convention delegates designated to represent a
local union held in receivership unless the delegates were
elected by secret ballot in a general vote of the membership.
This provision would prevent the use of trusteeships in order to control the choice of delegates to an international convention.

Except for these criminal provisions the law would be administered by the National Labor Relations Board in the same
manner as the National Labor Relations Act unless an international union chose to set up its own permanent independent
review board to deal with alleged violations. The qualification is extremely important. The Upholsterers International
Union and the United Automobile Workers have already established such boards voluntarily. Their use would preserve
the minimum safeguards established by the statute but
bring the administration closer to the people affected. Since
the necessary details of the proposal were explained in the

---

[102] S.3454, section 203 (c).

part of this paper dealing with the right of union membership there is no need to repeat them here.

The law cannot create the spirit of self-government. It cannot compel union members to attend meetings or hold their officers to a strict accounting. It cannot compel members to see in labor unions something more than service organizations hired to obtain benefits in return for dues. The most the law can do is to secure the opportunity for workers who wish to take an active part in democratic unions without undue loss of personal freedom. In my opinion careful legislation securing union membership to employees in the bargaining unit, guaranteeing fair elections, and curtailing the duration of trusteeships would increase the opportunity without weakening our labor unions or impairing their independence.

DAVID L. COLE

Union Self-Discipline and the Freedom of Individual Workers

MOST authorities who express views on the problem of protecting the rights and freedoms of workers use as their starting point the concepts of political democracy expressed in our constitutional system. This is presumably done on the assumption that we have provided legal measures to protect the individual in our democratic system.

Aside from the imperfections we see from place to place and time to time in our political society, one may well wonder whether democracy furnishes the ideal prototype for trade unions. Democracy's faults have been self-evident: We have seen political divisions and subdivisions in which leadership unresponsive to the wishes of the citizens has been perpetuated in office, with little or no practical means on the part of the citizens of selecting other leaders to replace the incumbents. We have seen people afraid to speak out on crucial matters because of fear of retaliation, despite the safeguards set up by law. The timidity engendered, for example, in the McCarthy era is still fresh in mind.

I question whether the forms used in constitutional government are necessarily good prototypes for the forms used in unions, because the nature, purposes, and functions of unions are different from those of government. As to the inevitability of imperfections, we must recall that Montesquieu, who influenced the thinking of the founding fathers as much as anyone else, wrote:

> If a republic be small, it is destroyed by a foreign force; if it be large, it is ruined by internal imperfection. To this twofold inconveniency democracies and aristocracies are equally liable, whether they be good or bad. The evil is in the very thing itself, and no form can redress it.

It is a helpful starting point in this discussion to examine the views of several people who have had experience in this field or who have recently made studies of the subject. I have in mind, for example, the book by Seidman, London, Karsh, and Tagliacozzo, *The Worker Views His Union*,[1] W. Willard Wirtz's address, "Due Process of Labor Arbitration,"[2] Clark Kerr's *Unions and Union Leaders of Their Own Choosing*,[3] and Paul Jacobs' article, "Union Democracy and the Public Good."[4]

Seidman and his coauthors believe that, by the test of responsiveness of leaders to the desires of members, most unions are democratic, at both the national and local levels, but that

democracy requires more than this; the essential factor is the ability of the rank-and-file member to affect decisions, to replace leaders, and to change policies.

Wirtz declares:

> There remains . . . in our thinking about due process a particular emphasis, even in the face of institutional interests, upon the individual's own, independent, even self-serving interest. The degree or forms of this emphasis may even be democracy's distinguishing characteristic.

---

[1] University of Chicago Press: 1958.
[2] Delivered at the National Academy of Arbitrators, St. Louis, January 30, 1958 (to be published by the Bureau of National Affairs, Washington, D.C.).
[3] The Fund for the Republic, New York: 1958.
[4] *Commentary* (January, 1958).

Kerr examines union behavior in terms of the prime functions that unions are performing and expresses the view that in achieving a better balance among the three power groups of our society—the state, the corporation, and the union—certain restrictions on the freedom of the worker have necessarily developed. He would not want this price for the benefits from industrial society to become too high, and one of the possibilities he proposes as a hope for democracy is a new faith to replace the old, traditional faith of the labor movement. This may lie, he suggests, "in the development of unions as a liberating force in industrial society."

Jacobs finds that the lack of conventional democratic procedures in unions does not necessarily lead to corruption or to the absence of a progressive social outlook; that in one union which he studied closely the constant use of the referendum and the existence of an active two-party system has still left that union

a conservative, and sometimes even a reactionary group, indifferent to political ideals, generally isolated from the socially conscious elements of the labor movement, and tolerant of work practices . . . dubious economically and socially.

These viewpoints bring into focus the complications which must be faced in considering whether union self-discipline can meet the problems of freedom for the individual worker. If unions are well established and secure, as Kerr suggests, then indeed it is now time to replace the belligerency and harassment of the earlier era with something else. Wirtz would give consideration to the interests of the individual, even as opposed to those of the union and its general membership. Seidman and his associates would strive for more power in the hands of the workers to achieve greater responsiveness and sensitivity in their leadership. Jacobs would stress the social responsibilities and activities of the organization.

No sound evaluation can be made without discussing the nature of the several interests and of democracy as a whole. As a political form democracy is generally taken to mean that the ultimate authority rests with the citizens, which they exercise through the selection of representatives to whom authority is delegated, and through their right to replace the representatives from time to time. Between such times, as we know, the citizens have sometimes suffered seriously at the hands of those entrusted with authority, but the citizens have retained the ultimate power to remove their representatives, and in the meantime the voters have had the benefit of certain basic safeguards which customarily go with the democratic form. These of course are mainly set forth in the Bill of Rights and in its counterparts in the several states. In unions the most important rights would be the right of free expression, including criticism, and of assembly and organization for the purpose of replacing undesirable leadership, all without fear of retribution. The fear of retribution is real; it has seriously impaired in many instances the exercise of the rights which the members explicitly or implicitly now have. The ability to exert pressure and induce fear has been a strong deterrent in some organizations. Union membership "in good standing" is an important condition of job security and opportunity.

What are the interests of the union? This depends on the state of organization. When workers are engaged in a struggle to establish a union and to obtain recognition, a solid front is vital. The picket line is sacred. Individual workers may not, without seriously hurting the group, decide they will take active steps to support the employer in such circumstances. To do so would be to exercise the dubious right of working at a gross disadvantage in relation to the employer, which, as history has shown, has reflected itself in lower wages, longer hours, and other inferior conditions of employment, and with no ability to review or participate in many decisions which affect them in terms of job security, promotion opportunities, and a variety of other matters. This, on the whole, has been recognized and accepted. Most problems with which we are concerned arise after the union has been in existence and recognized for some time.

We then come to the new stage. In the earlier stage the union, we assume, has become relatively secure. It has agreements with the employer, and it has probably been granted some form of compulsory membership to assure this security. It has probably also eliminated the gross inequities under which its adherents had been working, and has attained for them a sense of dignity and protection. The charge of exploitation against the employer would now have a rather hollow ring. Disputes will continue to arise over wage adjustments and improved benefits under the variety of plans in effect, but they will lack the grimness and urgent appeal of the earlier days. What, at this stage, are the principal interests of the organization?

The union will still seek to maintain strength and solidarity. It will do so because it will thereby have better bargaining strength, and because it is not certain how it will fare if, in a serious depression, the employer undertakes to weaken or eliminate the union, still dreaming, as John L. Lewis likes to put it, of the good old golden days. These are legitimate union interests, and for the benefits received the workers should be willing to forgo some of their individual desires.

The union may be one that believes it should not confine its activities to the work place. It may favor health centers, housing developments, resort areas, and perhaps a concentration on political affairs. These concerns are outside the limits of the essential purposes of a labor organization; the members' preferences, it would seem, are entitled to much more play and weight in these concerns than in the minimum and basic purposes of the organization. Provision for the free expression of individual preferences on such subjects must be made in any democratic setup, and those who disagree with the majority should certainly be given the complete right to say so, to take action accordingly, and to be free from any fear of retaliation because they do so.

A successful union is well mobilized and well financed. Having won its basic battle with the employers, it may turn its forces in other directions and expect the same unquestioned loyalty and obedience from its members as it had when it was fighting for existence. In jurisdictional disputes with other unions it sometimes seems that fully as much energy and vehemence are employed as in differences with management. If the struggle is to preserve the existing work jurisdiction or to resist attempted intrusions by other unions into the established bargaining relationships, it becomes difficult to distinguish between the group and the individual interest; in fact such struggles generally have the full support of the membership. Differences, however, may arise because of two circumstances: (1) when the union is itself the aggressor in trying to strip some other union of its established jurisdiction or bargaining relationship; and (2) when the union is prevented from prosecuting what it earnestly believes to be its just cause along these lines because of the restrictions placed on all affiliates of the AFL-CIO.

In the first situation, the members may well and properly differ with their leadership, and should be encouraged and protected in doing so. In the second situation we are led closer to the broad responsibility of trade unions. In this respect, there is less reason for going to lengths to satisfy employees who desire to follow a different course. After almost twenty years of feuding between the AFL and CIO, there was general accord, both within and outside the labor movement, that it would be most desirable and constructive to heal this breach. The protection of established bargaining relationships was found to be the first essential step in that direction, and the no-raiding agreement, buttressed by other agreements of similar purport, helped overcome the major obstacles to unification. The area has now been considerably widened. In February, 1958, the Executive Council of the AFL-CIO determined that under the constitution of the federation (Article III, Section 4, and Article II, Section 9) all affiliated unions, whether parties to any of the several jurisdictional disputes agreements or not, are bound to respect the integrity and the established bargaining relationships of all other unions. This matter is so closely related to the general welfare of the labor movement as a whole that I cannot conceive that individual worker disagreement with this policy should be considered one of the individual interests that deserves special protection against this policy of the union and the acquiescence in this policy by its leadership.

Bearing on this question of the individual worker's interest as possibly opposed to that of the union, are three types of union policy: (1) maintenance of the process of collective bargaining, (2) coöperation with the employer in the common desire to improve the relationship and avoid needless friction, and (3) respect for the group's obligations to the community, to other industries, and to the nation.

The first policy was at issue in the December, 1957, New York City Transit case. New York City Transit is a publicly owned and operated local transportation system, formerly in private hands. It was taken over when the private interests found they could not continue for financial reasons. Such publicly owned operations are excluded from the National Labor Relations Act as well as from the New York State Labor Relations Law, and the courts have repeatedly held that there is no duty, under the law, for the Transit Authority to bargain with or recognize any union. Until recently, the public agency accordingly denied its employees the rights customarily given to workers, with the result that worker morale suffered, and a strong spirit of resentment prevailed. In 1957 the Authority called a panel to advise how it could follow more conventional labor-relations patterns consistent with its primary duty to the public. It was advised to have an election conducted to determine which union the employees preferred. The suggestion of several organizations that the work force be broken down into subgroups of various kinds for bargaining purposes was rejected on several grounds, the principal one being that this would subject the Authority to many separate negotiations, any one of which might result in a shutdown of its essential transportation system. The disappointed organizations joined in strike, maintaining that they had been denied their basic rights under a system of industrial democracy. Curiously, while this was labeled a strike about the principle of craft unionism, most groups which joined the prime movers (the motormen) included within their individual coverage all sorts of occupations and combinations of crafts, skilled and unskilled, two of them being organized along straight industrial union lines. In total, as stated to the panel, these organizations represented a substantial part of the full work force. Nevertheless, they rejected offhand the recommendation of the panel that they should seek, through their right of expression and vote, to correct policies of which they disapproved; and to do so within the confines of the organization that might be selected to represent the employees as a whole.

Considering the history of labor relations in the New York transit system and the legal right of the Authority to reject or discontinue the process of collective bargaining entirely, one may question whether the individual interests may be indulged to the point where the essentials of industrial democracy may be seriously endangered or even destroyed; and where obligations of organized groups of citizens to the community as a whole are involved.

Some critics belittle the validity of the aspiration to create a more coöperative relationship with the employer. I believe, however, that the techniques used, once recognition had been securely established, are designed toward this end—that this is one of the hopes of our national labor policy. Some unions and

employers have made substantial progress in this direction, and
I am convinced that they are rendering a good service and
providing something of substantial value to their members in
doing so.

This leads to the problem of social responsibility—a problem that arises in public utilities, industries which because of
public concern may operate only under government franchise
and subject to government regulation and control. Disagreements over wages and similar matters, if carried to the ultimate point, have a direct and serious effect on large numbers
of innocent third parties. This may be at the local level, but
may extend to the state, regional, and national levels. Besides,
there are some industries whose peculiar nature makes them
the object of special public interest. Most typical would be the
atomic-energy industry, where, as in the New York Transit
System, the government plays the leading part. Other industries, although private in nature, are the sources of materials or
services on which many others depend, like coal, railroads, and
steel. A shutdown in one of these will quickly cause shutdowns
and layoffs of employees in numerous other industries, not to
mention the adverse effects on communities or areas as a whole.
Finally, there are times that are critical to the nation—when
a private dispute becomes a matter of serious general concern.

The attitudes of labor organizations toward such industries
or conditions have varied, from organization to organization
and from time to time. Participating in several such disputes
as a representative of the public, I observed that at the lower
union levels the interest has been more strongly in possible
wage or other improvements, but at the higher, policy-making
levels there has been greater concern for the public interest.
At critical times, serious shutdowns have been avoided or curtailed by enlisting the help of major union officials.

In the study conducted for the Secretary of Labor in the field
of labor-management disputes in atomic energy, the panel recommended that formal dispute-handling procedures be abol-

ished in favor of more active participation by important labor
representatives with the government officials in determining
which operations at which times could not stand interruptions;
the panel was convinced that such a procedure would result in
the acceptance of a greater degree of responsibility by labor.
In a similar study made for Governor Meyner of New Jersey
with regard to the special law of that state aimed at preventing
serious public-utility strikes, the recommendations of a tri-
partite panel were substantially to the same effect.

In situations where the public interest is paramount, how
does one measure the individual worker's interests when they
are asserted to be opposed to those of their representatives?
What *is* the individual interest?

Generally, it is his belief that he could get more money or
some other benefit if he presses the advantage he thinks he has
at the moment. If the policy of the union is to proceed along
other lines because of some of the considerations mentioned,
and a worker and like-minded others are unable to prevail
tactically, they may at this point complain that their individual
interests are being ignored and that they are being denied the
freedom to proceed as they prefer. That the course they advocate may be harmful to the union, to its relationship with the
employer, to the labor movement as a whole, or to the community or nation, these individuals may be willing to overlook
in the prosecution of their self-interest as they see it. The alternative, of course, would not be the surrender of the workers'
claims but the adoption of some means other than the picket
line to work out a settlement.

If individual worker interests are indulged to the exclusion
of all other interests, what reaction may be expected by the
public, and eventually by the government in terms of corrective legislation? What effect would such legislation have on
the fundamental processes and institutions developed under
our current national labor policy? Do the functions of the
policy-making leadership not necessarily include the evaluation

of the several interests and the determination of alternative
courses to be followed where the leadership conceives a strike
to be irresponsible and unwise?

I do not wish to be misunderstood. The narrow, materialistic
urge is by no means the only form of worker interest. There
are many situations in which crafts or groups of employees
earnestly desire and need autonomy. Their problems may be
of a special nature, and by tradition they may be fearful of
functioning as part of a larger organization. Groups may request autonomy simply because of the pride of an elite. My
criticism would be directed only at those who, unable to attain
recognition of their group by themselves, join with the broader
group to accomplish this, and then because of purely materialistic motives seek to break away without regard to what this
may do to the joint efforts of the others.

Where, however, regardless of the provisions of the union's
constitution or bylaws, workers are prevented from making
their voices or their justifiable criticisms heard, one could not
possibly find fault if they elect in some appropriate group to
go their own way.

We must remember, however, that the power of workers to
decertify their union or to associate themselves with some other
union is now seriously circumscribed by the no-raiding agreement and the provisions of the AFL-CIO constitution relating
to the protection of established bargaining relationships. The
threat of workers leaving one union for another has been weakened considerably, and in consequence a greater responsibility
must rest on the AFL-CIO to take effective steps to correct the
causes which normally prompt workers to seek relief through
such action.

This leads to the problem of corruption and despotism on
the part of the leadership. Can organized labor relieve itself
of such leadership? The record to date is spotty, although the
determination exhibited by the AFL-CIO is distinctly encouraging. I believe labor is now capable of accomplishing a great

deal by itself. The AFL-CIO is almost impotent, however, except in terms of influence and public opinion. The power of expulsion based on disclosures made by a Senate committee is exceedingly unsatisfactory. The emphasis on autonomy by some of the unions least deserving of it is a serious handicap to the officers of the federation, under its constitution. Indeed, the situation reminds one strikingly of the futility of the federal government under the Articles of Confederation.

The federation, for the protection of workers and of the movement as a whole, must be given authority to investigate its affiliates and their subdivisions, with subpoena powers, together with the right to examine books and records, and to compel corrective action for violations of its code of ethics or of law. It is unrealistic to expect local or regional union officers to search diligently for evidence of misconduct on the part of those with whom they are closely and personally associated. The federation must be given a greater part to play for the very purpose of better protecting the position of the individual worker.

I also believe that the prominence given the disclosures of the misconduct of several leaders of labor has encouraged individual workers to speak up, and that they will be less fearful about taking steps to recoup money losses or to be rid of corrupt leaders. I note, for example, that in the last quarter of 1957 more than 400 unfair labor-practice charges were filed by employees at the NLRB against unions. Union leaders who help themselves to funds of the organization or who take bribes are clearly liable for breach of their fiduciary obligations, and a few members with courage can activate proceedings in the courts through which relief could be forthcoming, under existing laws. They need encouragement and assurance from the federation and from the vast number of honest labor leaders who realize what harm such practices are doing to the entire labor movement. I predict that such suits will become more common.

In conclusion, therefore, it is my opinion that labor itself can do more to provide protection for individual workers, and can do it more quickly, than can possibly be accomplished through other means. If the constitutions will be reviewed and the basic safeguards of democratic practices plainly written in where they are now absent, this in itself will tend to improve conditions. With this must be coupled a delegation of greater authority to the federation to do an effective job of policing and administration. It has demonstrated that it earnestly desires to do this, but it has not had the necessary tools with which to work.

On the other hand, it must be made clear that the satisfaction of individual workers' preferences is not to be confused with their indispensable freedom. Rights in any society are relative. Employees who accept the benefit of group action have no absolute right to assert their interests as superior to those of the group or of the community or nation. If they demand the rights of democratic procedures, they may not deny these benefits to others, and particularly not to the majority. The one area in which they may demand satisfaction of their interests, irrespective of the wishes of the majority, is in the elimination or holding to account of dishonest or despotic leaders who in their administration of the union's affairs are violating the law or the fundamental rules of the organization.

It is sometimes hard to know what labor's critics are seeking. We hear the plea for the democratic expression of the workers' wishes when their officers threaten a strike or reject a proposed settlement. On the other hand, we see the officers taken to task for not exercising leadership and discipline when they are inclined to resolve some dispute while the membership has contrary views.

We must bear in mind that industrial democracy is primarily intended to establish equality in certain matters between groups of employees and their employer. Democracy is intrinsically tied to the principle of collective bargaining, and I emphasize the word collective.

When we explore the means of protecting the freedom of the individual worker, we must be aware that we are thinking of him within the framework of an organization that itself has a major function to fill on behalf of the workers as a whole. The union is expected to do an effective job in promoting the economic interests of the workers and to be socially progressive and responsible while doing so. To expect it at the same time to operate as though it were an anarchy within itself would seem to present an impossible dichotomy.

ARTHUR J. GOLDBERG

A Trade-Union Point of View

ONE of the more important legislative issues in the United States today is the extent to which federal legislation should be enacted, regulating in greater or lesser degree, the manner in which American trade unions conduct their internal affairs. Much has already been said on the subject by informed and uninformed persons. Much of the discussion on this subject has overlooked some fundamentals. Assumptions have been made which I think are erroneous. Insufficient thought has been given, I suggest, to the presuppositions which, perhaps unwittingly, color many of the proposals which have been made.

It is not my purpose to discuss particular legislative proposals in detail. I think it is more important to explore the criteria by which legislative proposals should be judged and the assumptions which should underlie any legislative approach to the internal affairs of trade unions, than to discuss the practical pros and cons of particular proposals. It is in discussion of these underlying and often unspoken assumptions that we come to grips with the real problem of labor organization in a free society.

Let me illustrate the distinction I am trying to make. It is often suggested that there should be legislation requiring a secret-ballot vote before a strike can be called by a union. Such a procedure was, indeed, tried and discarded during

World War II. Recently discussion of the pros and cons of this procedure has been renewed, particularly since President Eisenhower suggested such a provision in 1954. Little of the discussion has, however, investigated the premises on which the suggestion was based. The most important argument in favor of the proposal is that before a union takes action that will prevent workers from working, the decision should be approved by a referendum of those affected. This, of course, raises problems concerning the extent to which, even in political life, major decisions should be required to be made by a referendum vote of the electorate or should be permitted to be made by the elected representatives. Even passing this problem, the argument is based on an assumption which is usually not referred to and which is often not true—namely, that if the union decides on a strike, then the result will be that none of the workers represented by the union in the unit will work so long as the strike continues. This is true in some situations. It is most emphatically not true in others. Indeed, I think those who make the proposal that there should be a secret-ballot vote before a strike can be called would be repelled by the adoption of legislation which would state that the decision of the majority so made should be binding upon all.

The bitter labor controversies in the history of the development of union organization in this country have arisen from the fact that our law recognizes and, indeed, protects the right of an individual who, disagreeing with the majority on the strike question, chooses to work. One example is the Kohler strike. Those who have asserted vigorously the desirability of the secret-ballot strike vote have, it is true, urged that if the majority votes against a strike, then strike action by the defeated minority should be legally unprotected and even punished. They have not followed through, however, on the proposition, which seems to me to follow necessarily from their premise, that if the majority do vote to strike, the defeated minority should lose their right to work during the strike.

Let me use another example. In discussion of union democracy it is often assumed that the ideal would correspond to democracy as practiced in our political institutions. The discussion begins, as it were, with the assumption that in an ideal system the membership of the union retains its power to direct the fundamental course of the union's action by competitive politics. The absence of competitive politics at the international union level, at least in most American unions, is regarded as a symptom of a lack of democracy.

But is it true that we can uncritically transfer to unions the standards and criteria which we apply to governmental politics? I think a moment's examination will show that we cannot. One of the fundamental assumptions on which our political society rests is the existence of a common consent that it shall continue to exist. This is so elementary that it is often ignored. Our society can tolerate extremes of factionalism because there is no question that, whichever faction receives the vote of the majority, the government will not disintegrate. Republican can denounce Democrat and Democrat can denounce Republican because all are certain that whichever is elected, the republic will survive. More than that, there is the assurance that the defeated faction will accept its defeat and will not attempt to destroy the government.

Do such basic assumptions apply for a trade union? Sometimes they do and sometimes they do not. I think that again many of those who actively sponsor proposals to require the most rigorous type of free democracy in trade unions would shudder at the proposition that the workers represented by a union do not have the right to take action which would be denounced as anarchy if exercised in our political society. What is the equivalent in trade-union society of what would be termed anarchy in political society? The equivalent, of course, is the right of the majority to dispense with union representation at all. This is a right which, under our present laws, is guaranteed to all workers represented by a union. At intervals limited only by the necessity of some degree of stability in industrial relations, our law provides that employees can vote not to have a union. And on occasion they do so vote. Even before the law permitting this kind of election was passed in 1947, workers had a right to decide that they did not want the particular union which represented them but desired to have another union. They thus had the right to substitute one form of union government for another. While such a right, by constitutional majority, theoretically exists in political government, fortunately for the stability of our political institutions we do not engage in annual "representation" elections as to whether we should replace a present form of government with another one. It is nonsense, therefore, to apply to the internal politics of a particular union the same standards that we apply to political societies.

Of course, the legal right to dispense with the union and the legal right to substitute one union for another is not always the same thing as a practical right, just as the legal right to work during a strike is not the same thing as the practical right to work. There are industries in this country in which the existence and the status of the union is relatively unquestioned, either by the workers or by the employers. And some of the basic assumptions upon which our political democracy rests may perhaps be applied in such situations. But, equally, we have in this country many situations in which almost the contrary is true, where the great struggle is to organize the working force into unions and keep it organized, and where employer opposition is continuous and sometimes successful. And even where the existence and status of a union is unquestioned—as, for example, in the basic steel industry—it is unlike political government in that it cannot legislate by itself on the matters of primary concern to it—wages, hours, and working conditions. It can only make demands, and its success in achieving them depends upon agreement of the employer and upon the economic strength of the union, should the employer refuse. If there is analogy to political government, the analogy is to a political government which may simultaneously face uncertainty as to its continued existence, that is, face a revolution, and which is periodically at war. The constraints which by common consent we accept temporarily in the political arena when such conditions exist may perhaps explain and justify the existence of similar, although permanent, restraints in the practice of union democracy.

These examples seem to me to require that we examine, with great care, our basic presuppositions of the role and the status of a trade union before we venture to make a judgment as to whether government regulation of internal union affairs is desirable. Even if we assume that some governmental requirement of union democracy is desirable, the analogies I have suggested indicate that the particular function which the union institution occupies makes the easy transference of standards from political government of doubtful validity. But here it is important to note again that the application of these standards is based upon the assumption of the continued existence, indeed the necessity, of the union as an organized force in every employment unit.

In America, certainly, the law has never recognized any such union status. And this is why unions react so violently to the imposition of the standards of political democracy to internal union structures. As Professor Kerr has noted, unions were built as fighting organizations. Opposition to union leadership has often been termed, and perhaps correctly, a divisive force which tended to weaken the union in its attempt to organize or to bargain collectively with the employers. I am forced to disagree with Professor Kerr when he asserts that unions are now "established, secure, and accepted." This is simply not true. Perhaps, having the advantage of a little hindsight, I would say that his statement is as true as the statement, which he made at the same time, that the day of fighting the unions is largely past because of the existence of conditions of full employment. We do not have full employment, as we are all too fully aware today, and I suggest that any approach to the problem of union democracy which assumes full employment is an approach built on quicksand. But even in the days of the recent past when we did have full employment, the assumption that unions are everywhere secure and accepted, that their fighting days are over, both with respect to employers and legislators, was untrue. In the United States less than 30 per cent of all workers are organized, and many of our unions are still struggling, and sometimes unsuccessfully, to become established, secure, and accepted.

And even those who have achieved this status have no certainty of their position. A number of states in this country have so-called right-to-work laws. Now the premise of a right-to-work law is essentially in conflict with the premise upon which most proposals for legislating union democracy are based. The premise of the right-to-work law is that the union society is one which an individual is free to join or not join, as he likes. In the view of the proponents of those laws, it is not enough to insist, as our federal labor law does, that the unions' continued existence as the collective-bargaining representative of any group is subject to recall by a vote of the majority. The state also insists that even where a majority do wish the union to function as the exclusive representative of all, still the dissenting minority has an inalienable right to refuse to be a member of that society. Clearly, this approach is at war with an approach which insists that internal union government must be conducted with the full freedom and the full democratic processes which exist in political society.

Of course, one can turn that around. In their opposition to these so-called right-to-work laws unions themselves analogize their position to that of governmental bodies. Citizens are required to pay their taxes, the unions argue, and just so the members of a unit represented by a union who obtain the benefits of union organization should be required to pay their dues. If they make that analogy, it might well be inquired why they are not willing to accept the standards which are implicit in the analogy. I for one would be so prepared. The condition, of course, would not only be that there is no legislation which prohibits the union shop; the condition would be, I assume, the mandatory existence of the union shop. Contrary to what is sometimes generally supposed, the absence of a right-to-work law does not necessarily mean either the existence of union shop conditions or the presence of a stable, secure, and accepted union to which all members of the working community belong. But, if we assume such a situation, that is, if we assume a society in which collective bargaining is compulsory, in which there is little or no choice as to whether there shall be union representation, and in which all working people are members of a union, then it would only be right to insist, with the utmost rigorousness, that union internal government be conducted along lines which would at least approximate the standards of our political democracy.

On the other hand, where we have a society whose basic premise is that individuals, at least as a group in a particular bargaining unit, have the right to accept or reject a union, in which we insist that the employer has full license to attempt to persuade the employees that they should not have a union at all, and in which consequently very few unions have the assurance of continued status and existence which our political governments have, then there are serious questions about the extent to which it is proper to apply the standards of political democracy to internal union affairs. Again, to take the extreme case, if we knew that all unions were in constant peril of losing their positions, if we knew that all workers had ready access to a vote to decertify the union or to elect another union, then our concern with legislation to ensure internal union democracy would be very small. The right of the individual would tend to be assured, not by competitive politics within a union, but by competitive unionism or by the competition between unionism and nonunionism.

Our real problem is that we have a very mixed society. There are industrial situations in which the assumptions of stability and security are largely true in practice, if not in law. There are situations in which these assumptions are false. And we are faced with a practical problem as to what kind of standards for internal union democracy can be applied to all. The kind of permanent factions that are desirable in political democracy are certainly tolerable in a union such as the International Typographical Union. They are intolerable—as anyone will recognize who analyzes trade-union history—in unions engaged in the life-and-death struggle to organize and to obtain recognition and collective-bargaining strength. To insist that such organizations engage internally in the kind of political contests which characterize our political arena is circular, because it is an insistence upon the destruction of the possibility of their attaining the very status which makes this kind of democracy necessary in the first place.

I take comfort in the fact that we have this problem. Although I believe that it is only through unions that the individual worker's rights within his industry are properly protected, and although I, therefore, believe that the most desirable situation is one in which there are stable, secure, and indeed powerful unions, I take some comfort in the fact that in a free society the state does not decree that this must happen. Any organizer, of course, would like to have his organization done for him by the state. He would also like to have assurance that once the job or organization is done, it will not have to be constantly redone in order to keep his organization together. But state-compelled unionism is contrary to the notion of labor in a free society. The notion of labor in a free society, in which labor must organize itself and not have its organization done for it, necessarily entails great variation in the extent and the stability of union organization in different sectors of the economy. The difficulty of our problem, therefore, is a function of our freedom. We do not have uniformity in the status of labor unions because our unions are free.

The notion of freedom, of course, implies that unions are not only free to organize themselves but are also free to create the conditions of permanence and acceptance which make relevant the present questions about internal union democracy. Their freedom to do so again has both a legal and practical aspect—and the more important aspect is the practical one.

Here we have to introduce an element which I have so far ignored: the employer. The employer attitude toward union organization is more significant than is generally recognized. There are employers who accept the existence of union organization as an integral part of their operation. It represents the social apparatus by which a rule of law is developed in the relationship between the employer and his employees.

In this kind of relationship the collective-bargaining agreement serves not only as an arrangement, setting the cost of labor, but also as a method of introducing civil rights into industry, that is, of requiring that management be conducted by rule rather than by arbitrary decision. In this view, the collective-bargaining relationship is one in which each side, union and employer, agrees to accept a form of industrial government in which they both participate and from which they both benefit. The benefit to the employees is apparent. The benefit to the employer is not always recognized. Under this kind of system of industrial government, the employer has a right to expect from the union that (1) it will live up to and observe the rules so far as the union, *qua* union, is concerned and (2) equally important, that the union will see to it that every employee who is part of the bargaining unit will abide by these rules. So that if an employee objects to the settlement of a grievance made by the union in his behalf with the employer, then the employer can appropriately insist that a final determination of the issue has been made and that it is up to the union to secure compliance from the individual employee. Similarly, if an individual employee is dissatisfied with an arbitration award of a grievance, the employer in effect gets a commitment that the award is final, that he is under no obligation to negotiate any further with the individual employee.

The essential attribute of this system, of course, is the acceptance by the employer of the fundamental proposition that the union is, and will remain, the institutional representative of the employees, and that its decisions will be regarded as the decisions of the employees.

This kind of acceptance does not exist everywhere in the United States. It is not required by law, since it involves much more than the "good faith" collective bargaining required by our federal statute. Although the law requires recognition of a majority union, and good-faith bargaining with it, there are many situations in which the employer has the legal right, and exercises it, to disregard the union as the institution through which the employees speak and decide, and to appeal to the workers to overrule the union. The most familiar illustration, of course, is the strike situation. An employer has the legal right to operate his plant and to seek to break the strike by persuading his employees to work. He has the legal right to persuade his workers to reject a union and to vote against it in an NLRB election. And, in many industries, these rights are actively exercised. I need only point to the Kohler strike, to a great segment of the American textile industry, to many sections of the oil and chemical industries, to the communications industry, to retail trade, and to almost all service industries.

It is obvious that in most of these situations the employer attitude is a critical factor in determining whether the conditions exist which make relevant questions of compulsory union democracy. There are, of course, situations in which weak employers are at the mercy of unions. It matters not what the employer's attitude is—he has to take the union and what it says whether he likes it or not. These situations are comparatively rare, despite a perhaps contrary impression. Some of the Teamsters relationships with weak employers which received much attention in the McClellan hearings exhibit this characteristic but they are atypical. Much more typical is the condition in many of our basic industries where today management would say (if it could speak candidly) that if unions did not exist they would have to be created in order to achieve some sort of industrial government.

(An interesting footnote here is the strike by the International Ladies' Garment Workers Union which, according to *Fortune*, was "precipitated by the employers, who demanded more effective union policing of runaway shops that evaded union standards.")

In the institution of unions and the system of collective bargaining we have a system of voluntary government, not created by law or compelled by law, but created by free people, both management and workers, as a matter of choice. Where this system is established and accepted, the union is recognized as the collective voice of the employees—both worker and employer recognize, as a matter of course, that the decision of the union *is* the decision of the workers. No attempt is made to have that decision overruled or disregarded by the individual, just as in a stable political society the decision of the law-making body is regarded as the law, both by those who favored and those who opposed the particular decision made.

This does not mean that those who oppose the decision do not have the right to seek to change it through the established processes. It does mean that until changed, it is regarded as binding on all.

Where such conditions obtain, there cannot be the slightest doubt that a free society must insist upon the existence of democratic conditions within the union organization. It is no answer to say that the union is a private organization. Of course it is. But it is a private organization with power to make decisions, to legislate, if you will, on matters of vital concern to those it represents. Despotism in this kind of private government would be as abhorrent as despotism in a state which established by public law the wages, hours, and working conditions that are the substance of the collective agreement and in a state which, as well, assumed the functions of enforcing these conditions.

I am firmly convinced, therefore, that democracy within the union institution is essential. By that I do not necessarily mean competitive politics, as in political government, for reasons which I have already suggested as to the limits of the power of even the most stable and secure unions. Nor do I necessarily mean that legislation requiring union democracy is desirable. It is perhaps a common error, particularly among those of us who are classed as liberals, to jump unthinkingly from the proposition that something should be to a proposal that a law should be passed to require it. Essential to the concept of a free society is the notion that this is not necessarily so.

A free society means more than a society in which the people, through the ballot, retain the power to control their government and the familiar rights of freedom of speech, freedom of the press, and so forth. As it relates to the sphere we are discussing here, the free society, at least in this country, implies that within the economic sphere the state does not prescribe action but allows freedom to private individuals and, more importantly in modern times, to private organizations. The state does establish limits, to be sure, but within limits it permits freedom. And through the exercise of freedom and the interplay of private forces, the tremendous job of regulating our economic society is accomplished without the actual intervention of governmental force.

To say this, of course, is to say nothing unless we say what the limits are. Freedom to set prices, for example, is meaningless if a minimum and maximum were established as limits by the state, and so close together that the area for private decision is small. What, then, are the criteria?

The criterion cannot be that freedom is to be permitted so long as there is no injustice. Freedom, indeed, implies the existence of some injustice, for if the just course is always prescribed by the state, then there is no freedom. The view which I think best expresses the notion of a free society is that social needs are best met privately and without compulsion, and that a free society suffers a positive loss whenever a course of action is prescribed by governmental authority rather than left to the free play of private regulation. The fact that such a loss is suffered does not mean that there can be no regulation; it means that the injustice or wrong to be corrected must be balanced against the loss. And only where it is judged that the failure of private action and private regulation to correct the injustice or social wrong is so apparent and so serious that it balances the loss to the free society suffered whenever governmental regulation is imposed, is a case made for the enactment of regulation.

This is all highly abstract, I know. Let me give a few concrete examples. The easiest, of course, is what happens every day in collective bargaining. Under our system, the wages, hours, working conditions, and the whole system of industrial government implied in the collective-bargaining machinery are established by private agreement, not by governmental fiat. No one will venture to say that the result is always just or right. There are weak unions and there are strong unions. There are situations in which a labor surplus exists, union loyalty is small or divided, and the market is such that the employer can afford to do without production for a period of time. There are situations in which the opposite is true. Economic injustice—real injustice—can occur when too great bargaining power exists on either side. But we tolerate these injustices because, on the whole, their existence is the price of freedom;

and the alternative, government regulation of the terms of the economic bargain in each case, we would regard as more costly to the ideal of a free society than the cases of injustice and social wrong which do, admittedly, exist. We do provide limits, of course. The minimum wage is the simplest example; but the minimum wage is not intended to represent justice but, rather, the maximum limit of injustice which the free society will tolerate.

The very institution we are discussing—the labor organization—is a product of the free society. I have already adverted to the fact that there are large areas in our country where union organization does not exist, and where the system of law in the industrial relationship is entirely absent because there is no such organization.

I think that this is injustice—real and substantial injustice. I am sure, for example, that for every case in which a worker has been unfairly deprived of his job, or of membership rights in a union, because of arbitrary union action, there are literally hundreds of cases in which workers have been deprived of their jobs at the arbitrary whim of their employer, because there is no contract which limits discharges to cases in which there is just cause and provides a remedy by arbitration. Except for certain specific limitations, there is no law which says that an employer cannot fire whom he pleases or discharge whom he pleases, irrespective of length of service or equity in the job, in the ordinary nonunion industrial establishment. There is, in short, no legal protection of the "right to work."

I am not sure that I would advocate the enactment of a statutory procedure which would require all employers to justify before some governmental body all their actions in hiring and firing individuals, although certain specific reasons for discharge or failure to hire should be subject to governmental challenge, as in the National Labor Relations Act and in FEPC legislation. And, as I have already indicated, I do not believe that we should have governmentally imposed unions. We would correct instances of injustice, no doubt, but only at the loss of important values for a free society.

Again, of course, we have limits. The state does not impose unionism (and if it did, I may say that I think the unions would be worth little) but it does impose limits, both on the employer and on the union, as to the weapons each may use in the private struggle to attain, or to reject, the system of collective bargaining. The imposition of these limits was in essence the function of the Wagner Act. Taft-Hartley imposed other limits and, analyzed in this way, most of our criticisms of Taft-Hartley are that it went too far in intruding government regulation where the instances of injustice, although admitted, were minor, and thereby placed all unions in a strait jacket. But, neither statute ordered unionism or nonunionism. Encouragement, yes—in different directions by the different statutes—but requirement, no. Unions do not exist, and the collective-bargaining system does not exist because the law says they must. Government has, it is true, by the imposition of limits, created conditions without which unions and the collective-bargaining system would probably be less prevalent and less stable than they are today. But the system remains one of private government, operating within limits imposed by law, with all the variations in structure and strength which come from the development of private rather than governmental organization to meet a social need.

It is in this light, then, and on these premises, that I believe the question of legal limitations on internal union affairs must be considered. Of course, there should be union democracy; of course, an individual should not be expelled from or denied admission to a union except for good cause; of course, private organizations which participate in the making of rules, as vital to the individuals they represent as many laws enacted by political government, should be responsive to the wishes of those whom they represent. But these are not the questions. The real question is the extent to which there has been such departure from these standards as to require the imposition of governmental control.

There may be a sufficient showing of such departure to establish some limits. But I am not at all sure. I do know that most of the excitement in this area is synthetically generated, and not always by people who are genuinely concerned about the maintenance and strengthening of the collective-bargaining system—and who are therefore concerned that unions accept the responsibilities inherent in such a system. An easy touchstone, although not an exclusive one, is the so-called right-to-work law. For reasons I have already set forth I think that those who advocate such laws and at the same time want to enforce democratic rights within unions are, in this respect, anarchists shouting for the right to urge people to throw bombs. Or, perhaps more aptly, they are Southerners who insist and fight for the right to secede but who also demand, simultaneously, the right to vote against President Lincoln in his campaign for reëlection.

But the excitement, however generated, is nevertheless real, as anyone who has participated in the current legislative situation in Washington is aware. Our democratic process being what it is, there may be legislation. My plea is that sensible and thoughtful people, people with genuine concern both for the elimination of injustice and maintenance of our free society, approach that legislation with some of the broader considerations which I have urged in mind. Our objective should be to strengthen, not to weaken, the system of private law created by collective bargaining. We cannot, indeed should not, impose standards which will eliminate every injustice. We cannot and should not unthinkingly transfer to union government the standards which we apply to political government. Nor can we assume, as some assume, that unions are everywhere secure and stable, and that the fight for organization and recognition is over. We must accommodate our legislation to the broad picture; we must proceed, I suggest, not with the objective of prescribing a particular form of union democracy, but of placing limits within which the endlessly variegated forms of private union organization can maintain their independence, their integrity, their individuality, and their strength.

HUGH A. CLEGG

The Rights of British Trade-Union Members

THE history of British trade-union law is characterized by two main strands. The first is a series of court decisions which have used the common-law doctrines of restraint of trade and conspiracy to confine and repress trade-union activities. The second is a complementary series of statutes which have limited, and in some respects entirely removed, the jurisdiction of the courts over union affairs.

One consequence of this process has been to create a privileged legal position for the unions. In Britain the law plays a smaller part, both in internal union affairs and in the business of collective bargaining between unions and employers, than in any other industrialized country.

A further consequence is that, especially in recent years, doubts have been raised whether union members are adequately protected against the authority which their unions wield over them. The courts have been responsive to these doubts, and by a number of fine distinctions (which have rendered trade-union law an extremely complex and tricky subject for a layman) they have brought the law further into trade-union affairs than a cursory reading of the statutes would lead one to suppose was possible.

The most interesting cases in which union affairs have come

before the courts in the postwar years have arisen from the
expulsion of union members. The cases fall into two groups.
The first has dealt with the right of unions to expel members
unwilling to accept a transfer to another union after a resolution of a jurisdictional dispute by the Trade Union Congress.
The verdict of the courts has been that such expulsions are
wrongful unless the union has express powers under its rules
to expel in such circumstances. The second group, which
comes closer to the heart of my subject, has concerned expulsions resulting in the loss of the expelled member's job, because of a closed-shop agreement or of what British trade
unionists euphemistically call "one hundred per cent unionism."

There is a difference in terminology between British and
American unions. The "closed shop" as understood in the
United States is rarely found in Britain, where the words are
used to cover both it and the "union shop" when either exists
by formal agreement with the employer. "One hundred per
cent unionism" is the closed or union shop enforced by tacit
understanding.

The closed shop is not unlawful in Britain. An employer is
free to employ whom he chooses, and may limit his choice to
union members. Similarly, he may dismiss whom he chooses
(so long as he observes the conditions of the contract of employment he has made) and may choose to get rid of non-
unionists. In the *Crofter* case (1942) the House of Lords applied the test of reasonableness to the use of union strength to
enforce union membership and held that it was, in this instance, a proper "promotion of legitimate interests."

The first expulsion case which I would like to discuss is that
of *Bonsor v. The Musicians Union* (1954) in which the House
of Lords decided that the courts could award damages for
wrongful expulsion. In this context it had previously been
held that a trade union had no existence apart from its members, and a member could not claim damages for a wrong

"done vicariously to himself by himself." This added to the remedies of a declaration and an injunction to restrain union officials from barring reinstatement, and is important both because expulsion from a union which successfully enforces the closed shop (as the Musicians Union does) is likely to entail considerable financial loss, and because it increases the penalties against the union, thus encouraging caution in applying expulsion rules.

There was little doubt in the *Bonsor* case that the expulsion was wrongful, because the officer who had expelled Bonsor had no power to do so under the union's rules. Earlier judicial decisions had already made clear that the courts are willing to go beyond this to consider the correctness of decisions under union rules on expulsion if the rules admit some latitude in interpretation as does, for example, a rule providing for expulsion for "conduct detrimental to the interests of the Society." The ultimate power of interpretation thus rests with the courts.

What is less clear is how far unions can exclude the courts by providing that its governing bodies may expel "for any . . . reason which [they] deem good and sufficient" and that they "may refuse at their discretion to state any reason for their action." [1] Many now take the view that, given a continuation of the recent trend in legal decisions, the courts would be likely to regard it their duty to see that the rules of "natural justice" (procedural due process of law) should be observed, and thus that the charge should be known, a fair hearing provided, and a decision reached in good faith.

A second important case, *Huntley v. Thornton and Others* (1957), arose from the use of the closed shop by district officers to punish a union member whom the executive of the union (the Amalgamated Engineering Union) had refused to expel. Huntley's offense had been to refuse to take part in a

---

[1] *Rules of the National Union of General and Municipal Workers,* published by the union.

strike which he considered to have been called without following the procedures prescribed by the rules. Having failed to
secure his expulsion, the district officers persuaded union members to refuse to work with him, not only in their own district,
but also in a neighboring district, where a threat of withdrawal
of labor by his fellow members lost him his job. Thereupon
Huntley brought an action for civil conspiracy against the officers and committee members concerned. The court held that
(apart from certain of the defendants who had been misled
by the others) the defense of protection of legitimate interests
failed, because once the union executive had refused to expel
Huntley, the persecution of him became a personal vendetta.
Secondly it held that the defendants were not protected by
the 1906 Trade Disputes Act, which rules out any action for
conspiracy arising from an act "done in contemplation or
furtherance of a trade dispute" (unless the act would have
been wrongful if committed by an individual). This decision
was reached despite the inclusion of a dispute "connected
with the employment or non-employment of any person" in
the definition of a trade dispute in the law. Thus it would seem
that a further clause is to be read into this definition, limiting
the protection of trade disputes to those whose predominant
purpose is the protection of trade-union interests.

These two cases reveal the recent trend in British legal decisions to bring trade-union affairs under closer scrutiny and
stronger sanctions. It is possible, however, to draw divergent
conclusions from this trend. It may be held to show that, whatever may have been true in the past, the rights of trade-union
members now receive a healthy judicial protection. On the
other hand, a pessimist might argue that if so much is revealed
in the courts, there are likely to be many more cases about
which nothing is heard.

This second opinion might gain support from the consideration that the British worker (like other workers, I suspect) is

not given to litigation. In the shipbuilding and engineering strikes of March, 1957, most unions had not followed the procedures of their rules in calling out their members. This was because they held themselves bound by the decision of the Confederation of Shipbuilding and Engineering Unions to which they belong, and because there was no opportunity for time-consuming elections to be held. Following the precedent of an earlier case, *Yorkshire Miners Association v. Howden* (1905), it would have been possible for any member to seek an injunction from the courts to restrain the disbursement of strike pay. There were some three-quarters of a million strikers, and the membership of the unions affected adds up to about half the total membership of British unions; yet only one action was commenced, and that was dropped. This may be taken as a heartening proof of the solidarity of British unions members; but there undoubtedly were some union members who felt their unions had ignored their rights, but did not wish to face the trouble and expense of an appeal to the courts.

The only way to discover whether the trend of recent court cases reflects a growth in oppression within the trade unions is to look at other instances of expulsion or discipline. There is, of course, no complete list of such cases. Some are known, however, because newspapers are quick to report the employer who refuses to comply with a union request to dismiss an expelled member, and others because they have appeared important enough to attract the attention of students of trade-union affairs who have recorded them.

Almost all these instances fall into two classes. The first comprises those in which a trade unionist's fellow workers wish to get rid of him (and this was the origin of the *Huntley* case). Usually the reason is the breach of some unwritten rule in the code of the working group, frequently a rule limiting output, or a rule limiting earnings, with the same effect. The second

includes those in which the union has used expulsion to discipline the leaders of a faction in the union, often after a strike
has been called without the sanction of the union.

So long as the employer is free to dismiss whom he pleases,
there seem to be no good grounds for denying workers a choice
regarding those with whom they shall work. It might therefore be argued that workers would be justified in asking their
employer to dismiss a fellow worker against whom they have
a grudge, and even in striking to back their request; but it
would not follow that they had a right to seek his expulsion
from the union, especially where the closed shop applies, for
their complaint against him ceases when he leaves his place of
work, and the loss of his union card will prevent him getting
work elsewhere.

Unfortunately matters are not as simple as this. Under full
employment, groups and teams of workers can usually manage
to get rid of anyone whose company they dislike without going
to the lengths of procuring his dismissal. It is only when some
real or imaginary offense against the *ethics* of the establishment seems to demand his punishment that this procedure is
likely to be invoked. Then two ambiguities arise. Are the
spokesmen of the workers (probably the shop stewards) representing more than the workers in the establishment who
have a grievance against one of their fellows, or are they acting on behalf of the union? And is the offense against the in-
formal customs of the working group, or against the written
rules of the union?

The confusion goes back at least to the formation of large-
scale unions. Working groups had their customs before trade
unions began, and have them still whether or not they are
organized in unions. No doubt when local unions were formed
the working customs and union rules might be the same. But
this could not last. William Allan, secretary of the then Amalgamated Society of Engineers, was able to assure the famous
Royal Commission of 1867 that his union had nothing to do

with the many restrictive practices which they had heard were associated with trade unionism. He was able to do so with a show of honesty because it was not the job of the national union to enforce or take responsibility for practices such as these. On their own initiative, however, the branches and districts could, and they did. As collective bargaining developed, customs were translated into agreements, but only those customs for which the unions and the employers were willing to accept responsibility. Others remained unofficial, or perhaps came within the scope of the power to make bylaws, which some unions allow their branches and sections, and their writ ran because they were tacitly accepted by the employers without formal agreement. Much of the regulatory power of craft unions still rests on these sanctions, but they are not confined to craft-union membership. The enforcement of union membership itself relies on them in most British industries, as do limitations on output or earnings.

William Allan was not wholly honest, because he knew that the power and size of his union rested, at least in part, on the enforcement of custom by its branches. This is still true today. How can a union pretend that the enforcement of union membership by its branches is not its concern? British unions might be much less willing to accept responsibility for output limitations, but the decisions of the working group are still, at least on occasion, taken and enforced through the union branch, and the union is thereby implicated.

It is thus impossible to give a clear answer to the question whether the offense of the member who exceeds an output limitation is only against his fellows or against his union as well. In recent years the need for increased productivity has given output limitations the appearance of immorality; but like much public discussion on industrial issues this impression makes more sense in newspapers and speeches than where the work is done. To my mind limitation of output has exactly the same justification as limitation of hours, but with the compli-

cation that whereas hours tend to fall (in the long run) so
that any undue limitation on the employer will tend to correct
itself, output tends to rise so that an unduly restrictive limitation tends to become more burdensome. Consequently at any
time many existing limitations may be indefensible. Since they
are unlikely to disappear, the only protection for employers
faced with limitation is to negotiate output along with hours
and wages. If employers prefer to defend their rather shaky
prerogatives, then disputes will continue to arise in which
they are asked to dismiss employees who seem to them distinguished only by their virtue.

It is not easy to draw clear conclusions from this confusion.
There can be no certain moral rule on the rights and wrongs
of procuring the dismissal of a fellow worker. It may be justified by group interests, or it may be victimization. The in-
formal customs of working groups cannot be separated from
the rules of trade unions. It can be said, however, that unions
should avoid allowing their authority to expel to be used in
disputes which are primarily personal. In the *Huntley* case, the
distinction between the desires of a group and the purpose of
the union became clear once the union's executive had refused
to expel, and continued persecution of Huntley was properly
penalized. Where the union does not distinguish, the outsider
is hard pressed to know how to judge.

The second class of instances is more clear-cut. Expulsion
or lesser penalties have here been used to discipline factions
or leaders of factions. Those best known to me concern the
leaders of London busmen in 1937 and of London dockers in
1950, both in the Transport and General Workers Union, and
leaders of strikes in the London district of the National Union
of General and Municipal Workers in 1946 and 1947. Here
there cannot be a shred of doubt that, given the rules, the
punishment was warranted. Evidence was carefully collected
and reviewed to show that on many occasions the offenders
had broken rules. In fact the complaint might be that on these

occasions a handful of men were punished for offenses against rules which had long been broken with impunity not only by themselves but by many others.

Unofficial strikes are more common in Britain than in the United States. Most of them are small and brief, and are settled before the regional or national headquarters of the union is aware that they have begun. Others are covertly supported by the unions, or at least not actively opposed. This was more common in the years 1940 to 1951 (when strikes were illegal in Britain) than it is now, but it still may happen that a union sympathizes with the desire of its members to win some local advantage (such as the closed shop itself) which, since it is not conceded by the national agreements of the industry concerned, is unlikely to be granted if the claim should be pursued through the official negotiating machinery.

The third and most important group of unofficial strikes (though not the most numerous) comprises those in which the union is in conflict with a section of its members. Where union rules debar "conduct prejudicial to the union" or "opposition to the policy of the union" an unofficial strike of this type is *prima facie* an offense against the union. For many years past tens of thousands of workers have been guilty of the offense each year, but unions have been slow to use their powers. Arthur Deakin gave one reason for this: "It is true that we have power to expel members, and in extreme cases do so, but I don't think it would help to stop unofficial strikes if we expelled more people. It is much more likely that it would increase unrest. Once men are expelled the union can have no more influence over them. It is much better that we should maintain our influence rather than weaken it by expulsions." [2]

Expulsion or threats of expulsion have been successfully used to discipline relatively small groups of unofficial strikers.

---

[2] Interview in *Manchester Guardian*, 1947, quoted in V. L. Allen, *Trade Union Leadership* (Cambridge, Mass.: Harvard University Press, 1957).

Some years ago the Northern District of the National Union of General and Municipal Workers adopted this device and succeeded not only in getting their members back to work, but also in prevailing upon them to sign an undertaking to accept the union's policy and authority in the future. The larger the group, however, the less likely that the threat of expulsion will be effective, and the greater the danger that Deakin's fear of weakening the unions would be fulfilled.

It is as well for the liberties of trade-union members that expulsion cannot put an end to unofficial strikes, for in Britain this type of strike has become one of the main weapons of union members against official union decisions contrary to their desires—although a weapon that can be, and frequently is, misused. This situation is recognized by some trade-union leaders (indeed they may have led such strikes earlier in their careers), and that recognition may also serve to explain their hesitation to use disciplinary powers. Large-scale or repeated unofficial strikes, however, undoubtedly weaken union discipline, especially when they are fostered by a faction within the union, and thus the union must choose between evils. In these four instances it may be possible to question the evaluation of the two evils, but there can be no doubt of the guilt of the offenders under union rules.

Expulsion can, of course, be used to eliminate opposition within a union even when it might appear to the outsider that the complaints of the opposition are justified. These instances, however, in which the unions were slow to act and the offense under the rules was clearly established, offer some evidence that British unions do not grossly abuse their authority for this purpose. In this respect the Communist-controlled Electrical Trades Union has recently received much adverse publicity for alleged malpractices. There is good reason to think that its leaders manipulate election results, but not much solid evidence that they have made wide use of disciplinary powers to perpetuate their control. Suspicion that threats have been widely and successfully used does not amount to evidence.

Another possible abuse of union power where the closed shop exists is the use of that power to exact payment from members for the provision of work and from employers for the provision of workers. To the best of my knowledge British unions are innocent of this. One reason is that the closed shop in Britain is usually a "union shop." A second reason is that exclusive jurisdiction is not the rule in British industry. Where it does not exist, the officers and committees of a single union have not the power by themselves to give or withhold work or workers.

The conclusions of this survey seem reasonably reassuring. We cannot know that there may not be more petty local dictators in British trade unions besides Huntley's persecutors; we may suspect that authority is abused in our one Communist-controlled union; and the power of expulsion may sometimes be used against a worker whose offense is against his fellows rather than against the union. But evidence cannot be found to show that the liberties of British trade unions are gravely endangered by union disciplinary powers and the enforcement of trade-union membership.

If this is so, and if we do not accept the view (which is hardly tenable) that the intervention of the courts, or fear of it, is the sole explanation, there must be other sanctions to provide protection for liberties within the unions themselves. What are they?

The answer is not that British trade-union officers are entirely free from corruption or lust for power.

Most major unions, from time to time, have to dismiss an officer for financial dishonesty. Expense accounts are sometimes inflated. Election returns are not infrequently faked by branch officers, and sometimes by more senior officials. For the most part, however, acts of this kind are performed individually, for personal advantage, and not (except perhaps in the use of elections by Communists) for the advantage of a clique or faction. Of course our unions are not free from factions, but (unofficial strikes apart) factions usually pursue their purposes within the rules.

In most walks of life corruption is less common in Britain than in the United States. British trade-union traditions are longer established, and British unions have not had to face the problem of organizing newcomers from many different countries. Moreover, British unions, even before the spread of Socialist doctrines, constituted a movement of social emancipation as well as a powerful pressure group to protect the interests of their members. Even if the philosophies of the past have now lost much of their force, they still have their effect in the idealistic and sometimes ascetic values which they helped to foster.

For these reasons the pressures against corruption are stronger in British than in American unions, and it is more likely that the British trade-union officer who succumbs to temptation will act alone.

This explanation will not by itself suffice to convince the student of institutions. Before he accepts it he will wish to see how these pressures work through the systems of government of British unions. Unfortunately, however, these systems are complex and varied almost beyond comprehension. Accordingly, although I shall attempt a brief exploration of this field, it must be confined to the national executive councils or committees of the six largest British unions—which between them cover almost half of the country's total trade-union membership.

The standard pattern of such institutions in British unions is a body of members working at their trade who have been elected to office by an electorate of the whole qualified membership of the union divided into constituencies; but the major unions provide as many exceptions as examples of the pattern. Among their executives, for example, indirect election is as common as direct representation. A more important consideration is that several of them include full-time union officers. The largest union, the Transport and General Workers Union, does conform to the pattern in this respect. The executive of the National Union of Railwaymen includes no permanent officials of the union, but it so arranges its business that it is in almost permanent session, and its members rarely if ever see their own jobs during their three years of office. (They cannot be elected for a second consecutive term.) The executive of the Amalgamated Engineering Union are salaried as executive members so long as they are reëlected to their positions. In the National Union of General and Municipal Workers, the executive of ten members includes five of its district secretaries (the union's most powerful officers apart from its general secretary), and five "lay" (that is, unsalaried rank-and-file) members. The rules of this union, however, exclude full-time branch secretaries from the definition of permanent officer, and there is always one or more of these on the executive. The National Union of Mineworkers is a federal body in many ways and allows its constituent areas to choose their representatives to its executive committee from among working miners or union officers as they please. The consequence is that all but four of the present twenty-seven members so elected are permanent officers of the union. The Union of Shop, Distributive and Allied Workers also permits officers to stand for election to its executive. Of the present sixteen members, two are full-time officers, and one is a member of the union's office staff.

It is impossible for an executive committee of lay members, meeting only once a month, to carry out its duty of directing and controlling the work of its chief officers, when these are professionals, chosen by ballot of the whole union, and often figures of national importance. Such executives lack the knowledge, the experience, and the weight to match their officers. For this reason the executives of the Transport and General

Workers Union and of the Union of Shop, Distributive and Allied Workers (with its large majority of lay members) can be classed as weak. Executive committees whose members serve full time or are full-time union officers do not suffer from the same disabilities. Should their members be dependent on chief officers of the union for their appointment, they may be even weaker than lay executives, but (and here is an important difference between British unions and some American unions) this is not true for any of these six unions. The executives of the engineers, the miners, and the National Union of General and Municipal Workers are relatively strong for this reason; and the railwaymen's executive has raised itself to a comparable position by its manner of arranging its business.

Where permanent officers on the executive represent sections of the union with considerable autonomy, another point arises: then their strength in relationship to the national officers becomes the weakness of the national union, for they will take care to guard their sectional interests. This is a consideration of some importance in the government of the National Union of General and Municipal Workers, and one of the most potent forces in the affairs of the miners.

The theory behind the lay executive, so-called, is that, however upright and idealistic a full-time officer may be, the fact that he holds a full-time (and in some instances, a permanent) salaried post in the union is bound to make his interests differ from those of the members. Consequently he must be directed and controlled by a governing committee of members working at the trade and therefore not dependent on the union for their livelihood.

This argument loses some of its force when the lay executive members in our sample are more closely examined. Apart from the railwaymen's executive with its full-time expense accounts and the full-time branch secretaries of the National Union of General and Municipal Workers, most of the lay executive members probably spend more of their time on union business of some kind than working at their trades. Outside of the National Union of Railwaymen, however, most union business is the local affair of the lay members' own section of the union, so that their experience is different from that of the chief officers. In comparison with full-time officers, the bulk of the lay members' incomes does not come from the central funds of the union, and in those unions which appoint rather than elect full-time officers there is the further distinction that lay executive members hold their various posts in the union by election. For these two reasons they are expected to be more independent than full-time officers.

Even less is left of the theory behind the use of lay executives when their weakness is taken into account. Their members may have sufficient independence of mind to wish to protect liberties within the union, but have they the strength?

The theory retains some force, despite the weakness of lay executives, because these executives are not equally weak over the whole range of their functions. Let us take lay executive members at their weakest, in the National Union of General and Municipal Workers, where they sit alongside an equal number of the most powerful officers in the union. They are in a poor position to decide the policy of the union on the major industrial and political issues, and they cannot hope to determine the actions of the union's officers in their negotiations with the scores of employers' organizations with which a general union has to deal. On the other hand, these lay members constitute a special subcommittee to deal with the salaries of permanent officers. Here is something that they can understand and control, and they do so. There is no doubt that their control is effective; the length and difficulty of negotiations over these salaries is an obvious indication of this fact. It is, moreover, a commonplace that British trade-union salaries are not high, and the salaries of this union, although above the average, are by no means out of line with other unions.

I would suggest that a similar attitude pervades their decisions when the executive is called on to review disciplinary
actions of subordinate bodies, or to take its own disciplinary
measures. A study of these decisions leads me to think that
there have been few, if any, gross miscarriages of justice; and
the lay members are in a better position to exercise control
over these decisions than over policy or negotiations with employers. I do not mean that it has been their task to hold back
their colleagues from dictatorial excesses. The permanent officers may have had an equal concern to reach a fair decision.
But I think that lay members had fewer temptations to injustice, and were in a position to perform their duty as watch-
dogs of the members' rights if called on to do so; and this constituted part of the atmosphere in which decisions were taken.

If this analysis is correct, it can be extended with greater
confidence to the executives of the Transport and General
Workers Union, of the Union of Shop, Distributive and Allied Workers, and also of the railwaymen. There are, however, no lay members on the executive of the engineers, and
the miners have only an insignificant minority. It might seem
that their national officers and executives, both subject to the
same pressures and temptations, would have both cause and
opportunity to form a coalition to dominate their unions and
perpetuate their power. Wherein lies the protection of their
members?

To students of British trade unionism this seems a strange
question, for these unions appear to be in less danger of authoritarianism than other unions, certainly than the general
unions. The reason is partly the more vigorous trade-union
activity and interest among engineers and miners than among
other groups of workers. It lies also in other elements in the
government of these unions.

For years past a coalition of national and area officers has
dominated decisions on union policy among the miners, but
it has not attempted to use the machinery of the union to

suppress opposition, and has on occasion suffered defeat. On many issues there has been some division between the areas, and all areas support the right of an area to its own opinion. Moreover, there are councils and committees of working miners with wide powers in each area.

The officers and committees of the engineers have to stand for election every three years, or more frequently, and most elections are real contests. For many years no single faction has controlled a majority of the major offices. The districts and branches of the union have considerable autonomy, and its national committee (or annual conference) is a more powerful, and sometimes more unruly body than most union conferences. There is also a final appeal court to settle internal union disputes and disciplinary appeal. Its members are elected from engineers working at their trade.[3]

My argument, then, is that the structure of British trade unionism and the traditions of public life in Britain reduce the likelihood of gross corruption and misuse of power in British trade unions; and that this tendency is reinforced by the institutions of union government. There are abuses, as the *Huntley* case revealed; but they are not the rule. In some unions a few senior officials may be able in practice to decide most of the union's business, but they do not ride roughshod over the rights of union members to enforce their authority.

This argument leads me to challenge some of the conclusions of the excellent and stimulating study of the International Typographical Union by S. M. Lipset and his colleagues. Their explanation of the union's two-party system seems to me admirable and convincing; what I quarrel with is their narrow view of democracy. To them all other unions are governed by "one-party bureaucratic hierarchies" and

---

[3] The Transport and General Workers Union also has an Appeals Committee, which is elected by its biennial conference. A number of smaller unions have similar institutions.

this I cannot accept. No British union has a two-party system, but I should hesitate to describe any of those unions as entirely authoritarian. Moreover, since it is possible to distinguish the more democratic from the less democratic among them, party systems cannot be the sole criterion of their democracy.

It is true that political democracy is apparently unworkable without the aid of political parties, but this does not mean that party systems are the essence even of political democracy. To most citizens, the rights which a democracy secures—freedom of speech and association, freedom from arbitrary decisions, and so on—are at least as important as the opportunity to vote for and belong to political parties. We know, however, that political opposition and individual rights reinforce one another. The opposition would not exist without the rights, and it in turn safeguards them. It is a fair generalization in the modern world that the one cannot long persist without the other. They are both essential to political democracy, and those of us who value rights above parties have nevertheless cause to tolerate the follies of party politics.

The central function of trade unions is to provide workers with a share in those decisions of employers which most affect them, and to do this unions must create and protect a number of rights for industrial workers—such as the right to organize, the right to voice opinions without fear of dismissal, and the right to be represented in individual disputes. These rights are essential to free collective bargaining, and free collective bargaining protects them.

So far, then, we have a close parallel between the conditions of political and of industrial democracy. Free collective bargaining may, of course, degenerate into something approaching syndicalism or into a "deal" between corrupt officials on both sides of industry. For this reason it is important that rights within industry should be supplemented by rights within unions. If the worker is to have more than a formal share in industrial decisions, it is also important that he should have a choice between union policies, and this the party system of the International Typographical Union is admirably suited to give him.

Both in Britain and the United States trade unions carry on the business of giving their members a share in decisions on wages and conditions of work, and of defending their rights against employers and management, sometimes well and sometimes less effectively. Thus they perform the valuable function of democratizing industrial life, as Lipset and his colleagues readily admit. In their internal affairs, however, British unions provide a paradox (which I suspect is also to be found in the United States) of authoritarian policy decisions together with the protection of the members' rights within the union. In this respect, therefore, the conditions of trade-union democracy are not the same as the conditions of political democracy.

No British union could properly be called a one-party bureaucracy. The words are better reserved for the governments of Communist or fascist countries, and for the dictatorships of Spain, Portugal, and some South American countries where there is a single ruling party. With this comparison in mind, it is clear that the term cannot reasonably be applied even to the most authoritarian of the six unions I have mentioned, the National Union of General and Municipal Workers. Its members have relatively little share in the making of industrial policy, but, as I have tried to show, their union protects their rights both within industry and within itself. At the other extreme, the members of the Amalgamated Engineering Union have both their rights and a considerable chance to affect policy decisions—though perhaps less than the members of the International Typographical Union—without a party system.

There is one important consequence of the maintenance of the rights of trade-union members. So long as they are maintained the members cannot be wholly excluded from decisions on policy. Perhaps the most important example of this in recent British history is the reversal in 1950 of the support which had been given by the unions two years earlier to the Labour government's wage-restraint policy. The minority of 1948 became a majority in 1950 through the gradual process of branch votes and conference decisions in the individual unions. This took place without the wholesale replacement of trade-union executives and officers by opposition leaders, so that another of Lipset's conditions of democracy —the willingness "to move from a position of higher status, power, and income to a much lower one"—was not necessary for this exercise in democracy.

I cannot fully explain this paradox of rights without parties; my analysis is far from complete, and there may be flaws in my argument. But of this I am convinced: so long as the rights of the individual trade unionist are protected within industry by his union, and within the union by its traditions and institutions, trade unions should be included among democratic institutions. And a greater service will be rendered to democracy by discovery and strengthening of the elements in trade unions which protect members' rights than by seeking to provide trade unions with a mechanism for ensuring a real choice for their members in all major issues of policy. For most of the time in almost all trade unions, this is impossible; but trade unions are not thereby condemned to unrelieved authoritarianism.

JAMES R. McCLELLAND

Experiences of the Australian Labor Movement Under Governmental Control

In 1942 I was expelled from one of Australia's biggest and most powerful trade unions, the Ironworkers Union, which occupies a place in the Australian economy roughly corresponding to that of the Steelworkers Union in the United States. No Australian union has ever been so completely captured by the Communist party as the Ironworkers Union at that time.

The reason for my expulsion was that I had opposed the policy of the union. I had made what I considered legitimate criticisms of the union leadership.

I mention these facts to show that I was not expelled for such activities as "scabbing" in a strike or refusing to pay union dues, or giving confidential union information to the boss. I was expelled because I got in the hair of the ruling junta in my union. I was then driven from my job by the union officials' threat to picket the plant unless the other men refused to work with me.

I consulted a lawyer who was also an eminent figure in the Australian Labor movement, a member of the Australian national parliament and a vocal defender of civil liberties. Though he did not put it so crudely, he implied that unions were a law unto themselves in matters affecting their relations with their members. He did not believe I had any legal redress.

So there I was, completely isolated and helpless. It seemed that a man could be expelled from his union for opposing the policy of the Communist party and could be driven from his job with an antiunion stigma on him, and the law would do nothing to help him.

Soon after I joined the armed forces. In due course I was discharged, took a law course under the Australian equivalent of the G.I. Bill of Rights, and qualified as an attorney. My practice has been mainly in the sphere of industrial law and I have witnessed far-reaching legislative and legal intervention in what had previously been regarded as the sacrosanct preserve of the trade unions. In many cases which have reshaped our industrial law in recent years, I have acted for one of the litigants, sometimes on the side of unions themselves, sometimes on the side of individual unionists battling against what they considered union tyranny. I would like to present a (necessarily compressed) account of the Australian experience over the past decade of governmental and judicial intervention in the affairs of trade unions.

As a preliminary, let us take a brief look at the distinguishing marks of Australian unions. The future of Australian unions and of labor as a political force were drastically affected by the fierce conflicts between capital and labor in the 'nineties of the past century. The workers were badly beaten in their immediate demands in the great shearers' and maritime strikes of that period. But these defeats, far from setting Labor back permanently, gave an impetus to working-class organization generally and led to the establishment of Labor parties, at first on a state basis and later federally. For the understanding of the difference in outlook between Australian and American trade unions it is necessary to take into account the close links binding the unions to one of Australia's great political parties, a party which, both in the state and national parliaments, is always either the government or the alternative government. Australia's unions are almost all affiliated to the Labor party, they contribute most of its funds, and delegates from the unions are a decisive bloc in its policy-making bodies.

For many years, therefore, the state—the government—has been something which the workers regard as, at least potentially, their friend and ally. In one of Australia's six states, Queensland, Labor was in office from 1915 to 1956, with only one break of two years. In the biggest and most populous state, New South Wales, Labor has been in office without a break since 1941. In the other states and in the national parliament, Labor has not been in office for such extensive periods. But the fact is that most Australian workers look to governments for major improvements in their way of life— if not today, then in a year or two when Labor will be back in office. It has been by the action of Labor governments rather than by spectacular victories over the employers in strikes that the workers have won their greatest gains—in workers'-compensation laws, social-service and pension provisions, curtailment of the working week, annual leave and long-service leave. Broadly speaking, Labor governments have pioneered social reform and non-Labor governments have not found it politically advisable to turn the clock back.

The next background fact to be taken into account is Australia's system of compulsory arbitration of industrial disputes and the legal machinery which has been set up to implement it. Not only did the class battles of the 1890's convince Labor that it needed its own political party; coming as they did at a time of great sociological ferment, when the movement toward federation of the six independent states was gathering momentum, they also set our more earnest sociologists and lawmakers in search of an alternative to wholesale strike action and industrial anarchy. The idea of the state in-

tervening as umpire between capital and labor and having
its decisions obeyed by both sides won acceptance among
wide layers of the population, including those who were active in the formation of the Labor party.

The greatest fillip to industrial arbitration was the writing
into the federal constitutions, under which a federal government was established in 1901, of a power to make laws
with respect to conciliation and arbitration for the settlement
of industrial disputes extending beyond the limits of any
one state. Under this power the federal parliament in 1904
enacted the Conciliation and Arbitration Act, which has un-
dergone a constant process of revision, experimentation, and
reform up to the present day. Under this law a Commonwealth Court of Conciliation and Arbitration was established.
Its principal tasks have been to make awards regulating the
wages and conditions of particular industries, to interpret
those awards, and to settle disputes between parties to those
awards.

There has been and still is a continuing debate as to the
merits of compulsory arbitration; of recent years there have
been mutterings in Australia from some prominent union leaders about the superiority of a system of collective bargaining. We are not, however, here concerned with that subject.
It is sufficient to say that, although Labor (i.e., both its
political and industrial wings) has complained almost inces-
santly about deficiencies in the way the system has worked
and has, as a government, attempted to rectify those deficiencies, the principle of compulsory arbitration of industrial disputes by an industrial court has been accepted as one of the
basic tenets of Australian Labor.

It would, of course, be a misconception to imagine that the
Australian unionist, because he looks to Labor governments
to improve his lot and because he accepts, even though a
little grudgingly, the system of compulsory arbitration, never
resorts to direct, extralegal action to enforce his demands.

Australia's industrial courts merely prescribe minimum rates of pay. If a union is able to force an employer to pay more than the award, the courts will not prevent him from paying it. Compulsory arbitration is not a strait jacket but its general purpose is to impose rules on the contestants for a share of the national product which will minimize the social waste and human misery associated with naked class struggle.

To sum up these introductory remarks, I am seeking to present a picture of the average Australian unionist (and that means the average Australian worker, since roughly 90 per cent of industrial workers, and 66 per cent of all Australian workers are unionized). He is a man who, although he can be goaded into strike action, prefers and accepts certain traditionally established processes of law for the settlement of industrial disputes, and whose reliance on his union to protect him from exploitation is supplemented by a faith in one of the major political parties to advance the frontiers of social welfare and security.

Let us now consider how the system of compulsory arbitration has operated in favor of an increasing judicial intervention in what were once considered the purely internal affairs of the trade unions. For the sake of simplicity, I will deal primarily with the relations between Australian unions and the federal court which is concerned with this branch of my subject, namely, the Commonwealth Industrial Court.

The parties which come before the court in the hearing of awards and the settlement of industrial disputes must be registered with the court. In order to obtain registration as organizations for the purposes of the Arbitration Act, both employers' organizations and unions must comply with certain requirements. Among the most important are provisions designed to ensure that those who purport to speak for the unions in their relations with the court and other organizations, should in fact represent the union membership.

The law provides that the affairs of the union must be

regulated by rules specifying the industry in connection with
which it was formed, the purposes for which it was formed,
and the conditions of eligibility for membership. The rules
must provide for the election of officers of the union and its
branches and specify the powers of those officers and committees. They must also set out the manner of summoning
meetings of members and committees and of removing officers and members of committees. They must provide for the
control of committees by the members.

Moreover, the rules must provide that the election of officers shall be by secret ballot and must make provision for
absentee voting; the appointment, conduct, and duties of
returning officers; the conduct of the ballot; and the appointment, conduct, and duties of scrutineers. When these latter
provisions (i.e., those requiring a secret ballot, etc.) were
added in 1951 it was also provided that the registrar of the
court could, for unions whose rules were already registered,
determine such alterations of the union's registered rules (after
inviting the union to consult with him on the matter) as
would bring them into conformity with these requirements.

The rules must also specify the manner in which industrial
agreements may be carried out by or on behalf of the union,
and the mode in which the property of the union is to be
controlled and its funds invested; and must provide for a
yearly or more frequent audit of the accounts.

The manner in which the rules may be altered must also
be set out in the rules. It is further provided that no rule
will be registered which is tyrannical or oppressive or which
imposes unreasonable conditions upon the membership of any
member or upon any applicant for membership.

Moreover, the court could (until recently), upon its own
motion or upon application of a member of the union, disallow
any rule of the union which in its opinion was contrary to
law, tyrannical or oppressive, or which imposed unreasonable
conditions on the membership.

(The court has recently lost, as a result of constitutional technicalities, the power to disallow union rules, but this temporary gap in its powers will undoubtedly be plugged by the legislature.)

A most important power possessed by both state and federal courts is the power, upon complaint by any member of a union and upon holding an inquiry into the matter complained of, to make orders giving directions for the performance or observance of any of the rules of the union.

The law is, of course, altered, enlarged, or restricted not only by legislative amendment, but also by judicial interpretation. Judicial decisions during the past decade have enormously enlarged the extent of the state's watchdog activities in relation to what used to be considered the purely internal affairs of trade unions.

A few examples will illustrate the manner in which the Australian Industrial Court has interpreted the law that gives it the power to order the performance or observance of union rules.

In general, it will be seen that these decisions represent a drastic departure from the view that a union's domestic affairs are its own concern. Australia's courts have, in fact, used the law for the protection of rank-and-file unionists against arrogant and unjust treatment from powerful, entrenched union bureaucracies.

The lawyer who advised me in 1942 that I had no legal redress against a union junta which, in apparent compliance with its own rules, had expelled me from the union was probably right. He could not in the light of cases decided up to then have been expected to ask the court to read into that section of the law which enabled it simply to enforce union rules, a power to insist that any member charged with an offense against his union must be dealt with in strict accordance with the principles of natural justice.

But by 1951, when the same Communist leadership of the

Ironworkers Union attempted to dispose of another member who was proving troublesome in the same way as it had disposed of me, it discovered that the court's interpretation of its simple power to enforce union rules now stood in the way of such tyrannical practices.

I am referring to the now famous case of Laurie Short, who has been since the end of 1951 the national secretary of the Ironworkers Union but who was, six months earlier, in exactly the same position as I had been in in 1942—a man expelled from the union simply because he was getting in its officials' hair.

Short's case marks a turning point in the status of ordinary unionists in our country vis-à-vis their officials. The court held that the union's expulsion of Short was invalid because, *inter alia,* there was uncontradicted evidence that the union tribunal which tried and convicted him, was "biased against him, hostile to him, and opposed personally and politically to him." The court also found "that there was no evidence whatever upon which reasonable men could find that the charge made against Short had been established."

The legal basis of this decision was that the court's power to order a union to obey its own rules carried with it a power to order the union to act under those rules in accordance with the requirements of justice. A court narrowly interpreting its power might well have been content to say that it would not interfere, provided the union followed the procedures laid down by its rules. The court found, by the way, in this case, that the union did not do so, but went out of its way to state its additional grounds for upsetting the union's decision.

The court's interpretation of its jurisdiction under the power to enforce union rules was extended even further in another case in 1951 in which I was concerned. In that case the court held that, even though there was no specific rule in the union's rule book against the use of the resources and funds of the organization for the support of particular candidates in a union election, the court had power to forbid such use.

In its judgment the court stated that to use the resources and funds of the union in the way mentioned

would deny the right of such candidates as were not to be supported by the organization [i.e., union], its Committee of Management, its several authorities, its resources or funds, to the freedom and equality in their candidature to which the election rules imply they are entitled. The funds and resources of the organization belong as much to them and their supporters as to their opponents and theirs. It cannot be denied that the provisions of the Act and the regulations are directed to the end of having the management and control of the affairs and transactions of an organization reposed in a democratically and freely elected body of executives and administrative officers. So far as the organization is concerned every member, qualified under its rules, has the right to stand for election to an office. To allow the resources of the organization to be used in a campaign for his defeat would be a denial of that fundamental right. It would enable the existing executive, in whose hands the resources of the organization lie, to use those resources to defeat all opposition to, or criticism of, its will. It could result in a complete tyranny and a permanent denial of the democratic nature of the organization, which the Act and the regulations are calculated to ensure.

In the same vein the court has ruled that the use of the union's journal to support the candidature of incumbent officials is a breach of union rules; and, on the other hand, the court has disallowed a rule prohibiting the issuing of circulars by members commenting on the affairs of the union.

The type of question which the Industrial Court is called upon to decide in its role of watchdog of union democracy is well illustrated by the case of *Byrnes v. Federated Ironworkers Association* which was decided in 1957. When the Communists were ousted from control of the Ironworkers' Union, the new officials who had been elected by overwhelming majorities in the first honest elections held in the union for

years found that the Communists in the union still attempted
to frustrate the will of the majority of members by the tactic
of controlling branch meetings and attempting to give directives from those meetings to the elected officials. In Australia
it is not easy to persuade unionists to attend the routine meetings of their unions. There are many factors working against
large attendances at such meetings. The result is that even
in a union where the Communists and their fellow-travelers
may not have the support of more than 5 per cent of the
members they can frequently get more than 50 per cent of the
votes at a routine union meeting. In a particularly glaring case
a branch meeting of the Ironworkers' Union attended by about
50 members instructed the officials to call a strike affecting
15,000 members, even though an overwhelming majority of
those 15,000 members had voted against strike action in a
plebiscite. To cope with this sort of absurdity the union
altered its rules so as to provide that directives from branch
meetings were not binding on the officials unless at least 15
per cent of the membership had attended. This rule was so
effective in countering the tactic I have mentioned that a
Communist supporter in the union ultimately challenged the
rule in the Industrial Court. The court decided that the rule,
far from infringing the democratic requirements of the Arbitration Act, was a democratic safeguard against government
of the union by tiny, organized minorities.

One other feature of Australia's industrial legislation merits
brief mention. It will be appreciated that a person who seeks
to challenge his union's conduct in the courts is at a great
financial disadvantage. Cases are often lengthy and costly. Industrial legislation therefore provided that a member of a
union who proposes to take proceedings for disallowance of
union rules or for orders directing the union to perform and
observe its rules may apply to the registrar of the court for
financial assistance. If it appears to the registrar that there
are reasonable grounds for taking the proceedings and that

the proceedings are proposed to be taken in good faith, he may direct that financial assistance shall be given by the government.

This provision was not introduced until 1949, and it is significant that the vast majority of cases of the type I have been referring to have occurred since that date. This provision, in fact, brought the democratic safeguards of our industrial legislation out of the realm of theory into the world of reality. As much as anything else it helped to put the ordinary unionist on an equal footing with the officials of his union.

The most controversial section of my subject concerns the intervention by Australia's courts and by the state itself in the conduct of union elections. It is necessary to take a brief look at the background to the legislation that made this intervention possible. Immediately before, during, and after World War II, the Communist party of Australia, by bold, astute, and unscrupulous methods, won for itself a position of control in the Australian unions out of all proportion to its numerical or electoral strength. Even in the rosiest days of the wartime honeymoon between the democracies and the Soviet Union, when it was almost respectable to be a Communist, reliable estimates place the top figure of the Australian Communist party at no more than 20,000. Yet in 1945 the Communists controlled most of the maritime unions, most unions associated with the mining industry, all important metal-trades unions, the most important unions in the building industry and in sea and land transport, and had a majority on the governing body of the Australian trade-union movement, the Australian Council of Trade Unions. This dangerous situation persisted into the first years of the cold war, and the alarm which it engendered was as strong in the Labor and trade-union movement as in any section of the community. The question on everyone's lips was: how did it happen? How did this small minority party get a stranglehold on our major unions and thus come so close to getting a stranglehold on the country? Part of the answer was: by crooked manipulation of union‧ballots. This seemed to be a reasonable explanation because the Australian workers were never pro-Communist and it did not seem likely that they would vote Communists into office in union after union. But there was no evidence to support this vague suspicion until a prominent Communist defector named Sharpley made detailed accusations of ballot-rigging in union elections which he said had been masterminded by the Communist party.

There is, by the way, no law disqualifying a Communist from being a member of a union or from holding union office in Australia. The law provides that a person employed in an industry, unless he is of generally bad character, is entitled to be admitted to membership of the union covering his calling and to remain a member so long as he complies with its rules. But this provision does not apply to a person who has, within one year of applying for membership in a union, advocated the forcible overthrow of the government. It might be argued that this exclusion would cover Communists, but in practice it would be very difficult to prove that a Communist, using the propaganda jargon which they use today, had advocated the forcible overthrow of the government. In any event I know of no applicant for union membership being excluded on this ground from a union, although there is a well-known case of a Communist being unable to regain admission to a union from which he had resigned because he could not prove that he was not of generally bad character.

Indeed, this very question of the right of Communists to hold union office was the subject of a referendum to alter the Australian constitution. Shortly after the present federal government, which is a non-Labor government, was elected to office late in 1949, it introduced a law to make possible the removal of Communists from union office and to forbid their holding union office in the future. This law was immediately challenged in the Australian High Court, which held it to be unconstitutional. The government then introduced a referendum to amend the constitution by endowing the federal parliament with this power, but the referendum was defeated.

1949 was indeed a climacteric year in the history of Australian unionism. In that year the Communist party, emboldened by its unprecedented successes in the capture of some of our most important unions, badly overreached itself. Through its control of the miners' union it declared a nation-wide coal strike, and with the support of the other Communist-controlled unions threatened to bring the whole economy to a standstill. Australian industry was then, even more so than it is today, heavily dependent on coal as a source of power, and because of the increased demand for coal and the limitation of the work force during the war, there were no reserves of coal for industry to fall back on. It was not long before the major steel plants and much of heavy industry were closed down by the cessation of coal supplies.

This was a situation which no self-respecting government could tolerate. There was a federal Labor government in office at the time under Prime Minister Ben Chifley. It was a highly popular government, which enjoyed the full confidence of the non-Communist workers. Chifley accepted the challenge and even resorted to the use of troops. With the backing of non-Communist unions he smashed the strike in a few weeks. All the Communists had achieved was to give further impetus to the movement which was already underway to whittle down their power in the unions.

It is significant that it was a Labor government which took the first step along the road of court intervention in union ballots. In 1949, the same year as the coal strike, Chifley's attorney general, Dr. Evatt, introduced a new section into the Arbitration Act. This section provides that when a member of a union charges irregularities in a union election, he may lodge an application for an inquiry by the Industrial Court. The application may be lodged either before the completion of the election or within six months of its completion. The applicant has to set out the facts on which he relies and, if the registrar of the court is satisfied that there is a *prima facie* case for an inquiry, he refers the matter to the court and an inquiry is held. The court is empowered to inspect and take possession of ballot papers (which now have to be preserved, on pain of severe penalties, for twelve months after an election is concluded) and enter premises occupied by the union. Severe penalties were enacted for any obstruction to the court's processes. At any time after the inquiry is instituted, the court may order that no further steps be taken in the ballot, or that a person claiming to have been elected should not assume office, or that a person who previously held office should continue to hold office. If the court, after its inquiry, finds that an irregularity has occurred, it may declare the election void and order another election to be held with whatever safeguards the court considers necessary under an independent returning officer acting in conjunction with the union returning officer.

It is expressly provided that the court shall *not* declare an election void unless it is of the opinion that, having regard to the irregularity found, and any circumstances giving rise to a likelihood that similar irregularities may have occurred, the result of the election may have been affected by irregularities.

Here again the Australian legislature has taken into account the fact that the availability of legal remedies is not of much use to a rank-and-file unionist if he can't afford the cost of pursuing those remedies. It has therefore provided that where, upon an inquiry, the court finds an irregularity has occurred in a union election, the attorney general may authorize payment by the government to the person who applied for an inquiry of the whole or part of his costs. Even if the court does not find an irregularity but certifies that the person who applied for the inquiry acted reasonably in so applying, the attorney general may still authorize payment of his costs by the government.

The same amendment also provided that a union, or a branch of a union, may ask the registrar of the Industrial Court to conduct its ballots. Several unions have availed themselves of this provision, and when they do so it is customary for the registrar to hand the conduct of the ballot to the electoral officer, who also conducts parliamentary ballots.

Finally, this particular amendment of the law laid down a list of offenses in connection with union elections and provided penalties for their breach of a fine and imprisonment for twelve months. These offenses include impersonating another person to secure a ballot paper, forging a nomination paper or ballot paper, destroying ballot papers, threatening or intimidating a candidate or a voter.

This major amendment of the industrial law was enacted, not by a government which could be said to be reacting to pressure from employers, but by a Labor government which was, in fact, reacting to pressure from the rank and file of the unions, many of whom had come to think that control of their unions was passing from their hands into those of entrenched bureaucracies and unscrupulous ballot riggers.

This legislation had an immediate and dramatic vindication. In the very year that it was enacted, 1949, Laurie Short ran for national secretary of the Ironworkers' Union. He was declared defeated by the well-known Communist, Thornton, by roughly 2,000 votes. Short challenged the result under the new legislation. The ensuing inquiry was a most exhaustive affair, which, with various adjournments and interruptions, was before the court for about 18 months. Finally, toward the end of 1951, the court found that there had been wholesale forgery and falsification in the ballot and declared Short to be the rightful national secretary of the union. Shortly afterward, in a national ballot in the union conducted by the Commonwealth electoral officer, the members showed that the court had been right, by reëlecting Short with a 2 to 1 majority.

This was a spectacular beginning for the ballot-inquiry legislation. But there have been surprisingly few ballot inquiries since. The reasons are not hard to find. The ironworkers' ballot which was upset by the court was a particularly clumsy fraud. To illustrate this, it is only necessary to mention that impressions on hundreds of ballot papers proved conclusively that they had been completed by the same hand from the same stack of papers. But the very crudity of this performance served as a lesson to would-be cheats in the future. After all, a dishonest union bureaucracy, if it conducts its ballot-rigging with skill and circumspection, has an excellent chance of getting away with it. Where the prize is great and the risk involved in defending it is small, the temptation to cheat under the pressure of possible defeat may become irresistible. I believe there has been a fair amount of cheating in union ballots in Australia, and in most cases I do not believe a ballot inquiry by any court would have uncovered the malpractices involved. This belief has been shared by more sophisticated trade unionists for many years.

The ironworkers' ballot case had a two-fold effect: it served as a warning to ballot riggers to be more circumspect in the future; and it proved for the first time and in a spectacular way that the general suspicion surrounding union ballots was not without foundation.

So people began to say: Why give them a chance to cheat? Why wait until a union ballot is over and then give would-be challengers the herculean task of proving it was fraudulent? Why not put the fairness of union ballots beyond question by having them conducted by an independent authority?

This proposal was on the whole greeted unenthusiastically by the official union movement. I do not suggest that all of this opposition was dishonest. Undoubtedly many union officials who considered they had nothing to fear from the free

expression of their members' wishes honestly believed that
the independence of the trade unions was threatened by the
proposition that union elections should be taken completely
out of the hands of the unions themselves. There were of
course also quite a few union officials, and not all of them
Communists, who opposed the proposal for the simple reason that they knew honest union elections would be highly
dangerous and perhaps fatal to them. On this issue we saw
some strange alliances of Communists with "right-wing reac-
tionaries."

The question became one of the important issues of the
national parliamentary election that was fought late in 1949.
In this election the Labor party was defeated and a Liberal
government, which has been in office ever since, was elected.

The new government did not go the whole distance by
taking union elections entirely out of the unions' hands; but by
an ingenious amendment of the industrial law in 1951 it
made further inroads into the unions' control over their own
ballots which had already been breached by the ballot-inquiry
legislation.

The Labor party's amendment of the law had provided that
a union, or a branch of a union, could ask the registrar of the
Industrial Court to take over the conduct of the union's ballot.
The Liberal government's further amendment provided that
such a request could be made not only by the union's committee of management, but also by a prescribed number of
the rank and file of the union.

The prescribed number was fixed at 500 for union branch
elections and 1,000 for national elections. Thus, for the first
time in the history of Australian unionism, a group of rank-
and-file unionists could, if they suspected that a union ballot
would not be fairly conducted, take that ballot out of the
hands of their union officials and place it in the hands of a
government agency.

This has been a hot political issue in Australia for the past

seven years. There has been a major split in the Labor movement in the past decade over the question of communism, and
how to deal with it in the unions. As I mentioned earlier, the
Communists managed to acquire a position of strength in
the unions out of proportion to their electoral strength. This
usurpation of union power by an antidemocratic minority
has provided the main impetus to the legislative and judicial
innovations with which I have been dealing. But the Communists, after severe initial reverses, have fought back cleverly
and effectively. Around the question of government intervention in union affairs they have managed to gather allies in
unexpected places. And the Labor movement has split down
the middle over this and allied questions.

The question with which we are concerned here, namely
to what extent governmental and judicial interference in the
affairs of trade unions is consistent with the freedom of the
trade unions and of trade unionists, is, of course, not necessarily connected with the question of communism. I understand that the problem of communism in American trade
unions is a negligible one but, despite that, the question of governmental and judicial intervention in the affairs of American
unions is one of the real and pressing questions of today. In
Australia, however, as a matter of history, the two questions
have been and still are inextricably interwoven. It is extremely
doubtful that there would have been as yet any large-scale
intervention by governments or courts in the internal affairs
of trade unions if the need for such intervention had not been
spotlighted by Communist usurpation of some of the highest
union posts and by their corrupt and tyrannical abuse of
union office.

The Labor movement reached its highest point of alert-
ness and awareness to the Communist menace during and
immediately after the coal strike of 1949. Most of the heaviest
blows against Communist control of Australian unions were
struck in the three or four years immediately after the coal

strike. Under the impact of the legislation of 1949 and 1951 and the organization in Communist-controlled unions of industrial groups enjoying the patronage of the Labor party, the Communists sustained heavy defeats in the unions and many of the most important Communist figures just disappeared from the industrial scene. I referred earlier to the close integration of unions and Labor party. As a consequence of this, a large-scale change of control of the unions produced an alteration of the balance of forces in the highest councils of the Labor party. This in turn led to a bitter factional struggle for control of the Labor party which had overtones of religious sectarianism and collaboration between Communists and important Labor leaders.

The Communists received timely aid from the late Senator McCarthy. In common with the rest of the Western world Australia watched, at first with alarm and foreboding but ultimately with relief and admiration, the contest in the United States between democratic institutions and the forces of McCarthyism. Australian Communists, of course, proclaimed McCarthyism to be the true face of American capitalism and equated McCarthyism with anticommunism.

These currents affected the political mood of all democracies, not the least Australia. McCarthy did a great service to Australia's Communists. In the context of the struggle which was then being waged for control of the Labor party, it was a great help to the Communists to be able to brand anticommunism as McCarthyism. And as the campaign for independent control over the internal affairs of trade unions had been waged under the banner of anticommunism, the McCarthyist smear was extended to cover all advocacy of outside intervention in the affairs of trade unions.

I do not want to give the impression that Communists control the Australian Labor party. But at all times they exert some influence on it—through secret Communists joining the Labor party, through union representation on the Labor party's governing bodies, through the impact of Communist propaganda on fellow travelers and anti-anti-Communists who form a fairly substantial proportion of the Labor party membership. On a given issue, such as the present one, they may succeed, at least for a time, in imposing *their* policy on the Labor party under the guise of some liberal-sounding principle. As of now, official Labor's attitude toward governmental and judicial intervention in the internal affairs of trade unions is closer to that of the Communists than it has been since before the coal strike of 1949.

Where do the rank-and-file members of the unions stand on the question? I mentioned that the present government extended the legislation pioneered by a Labor government by making it possible for rank-and-file unionists to take the conduct of union elections out of the hands of their union officials. There is no evidence of any widespread disapproval by unionists of this legislation. On the contrary, in most union elections in which a faction in the union has availed itself of this legislation and had the election conducted by the government electoral officer, that faction has been successful in the ensuing election. One would expect unionists who were against government intervention in union affairs to demonstrate their opposition by voting against a faction which invited that intervention. In most cases, they have not done so, even though they have been noisily invited to do so by those opposing government intervention.

The Communists, of course, who have been the main losers from fair elections, claim that the results in government-controlled union elections are faked. Now and then, however, this claim gets a severe blow when a Communist wins an election conducted by the Commonwealth electoral officer or when there is a mixed result. No disinterested person sincerely believes that union elections conducted by the government electoral officer are anything but scrupulously fair; and that is all that the average unionist is concerned about.

However, because the legislation providing for government-controlled ballots on request of a certain number of rank-and-file unionists was introduced by the political opponents of Labor, because it was introduced primarily to help unionists rid themselves of unwanted Communist officials, and because the Communists have been able to persuade the most influential figures in the Labor party that anticommunism is reactionary, I believe that the Labor party, if returned to office, would repeal this legislation. The Labor party would perhaps not like it that this is made an issue in a political campaign, because, as I believe, public opinion is in favor of the legislation. But once in office it would be under considerable pressure from a large section of trade-union officials—and not all of them Communists, by any means—to hand back to them control over their own elections.

However, I do not believe that a Labor government would retreat to a position of no state interference in union affairs. The notion that the control of unions with thousands of members and huge assets is an extralegal province of no concern to the rest of society is no longer seriously advanced in Australia by anybody who accepts democratic standards. The Communists alone are excluded from that category. A Labor government, I believe, would retain the legislation which it introduced in 1949.

I do not presume to generalize from the Australian experience and pronounce universal nostrums in this field. The emphasis undoubtedly shifts in different periods and in different countries. In the early days of trade unionism, when combinations of employees for their mutual protection were adjudged by the British courts to be unlawful conspiracies in restraint of trade, human progress and the cause of freedom undoubtedly demanded greater freedom for the unions from the shackles of the state and its instrumentalities. Similarly, in the totalitarian countries of today, a reduction, not an increase, of state interference in the affairs of trade unions, should be the slogan of freedom lovers.

But in the political and economic context of my own country, I for one believe that individual freedom has been advanced, not curtailed, by the increasing intervention of the state and its courts which we have witnessed over the past decade in the affairs of Australian trade unions.

The dangers to the freedom of the unions, which are painted in such glaring colors by the opponents of this increasing superintendence of unions by society as a whole, are, in my view, not to be feared by people with a real faith in the strength of democratic institutions. If we accept the rule of law in such spheres as the interpretation of our constitution, the protection of property, the safeguarding of the interests of shareholders in public companies, matrimonial relations, the rights of succession, why should we not accept the rule of law in the regulation of relations between union members and union management? If we are prepared to entrust to government servants the conduct of elections to decide who shall run our society, why should we balk at allowing the same government servants to conduct elections to decide who shall run our unions?

In Australia, at least, I believe that the unions are strong enough to protect themselves against any attack, whether from a reactionary government—if such a government could gain power in Australia—or from employers. But I believe that the maintenance of that strength depends in the final analysis on the belief of the individual unionist that his union is really *his* union. If he begins to believe that it belongs to a clique over which he has no real control he will not be greatly interested in the fate of his union if it should come under a real attack.

I have heard all the arguments against state intervention in the affairs of trade unions. As applied to the conditions of my country these arguments fall into one or other of the following categories:

1. They are the arguments of interested office-holders, who can hardly be said to be above the battle.

2. They are the propaganda of Communists, whose pretensions to care for the freedom of trade unions or trade unionists collapse before the example of Soviet trade unions.

3. They are the pious clichés which always clutter up the arena whenever freedom is mentioned.

4. They are the battle cries of a political party out of office.

The situation in the United States may be quite different. Perhaps in this country freedom demands that the stress should still be placed on the independence of the trade unions from control by the state and its instrumentalities. In my experience, as a unionist and a lawyer, it is emphatically not so in Australia. I should not like to see the trend of recent years reversed in my country. I believe that today the Australian unionist's freedom is far more secure than mine was back in 1942.

SUMMARY

THE most striking fact about the Arden House Conference was the organic character of the discussion. A session that began, for example, by considering a specific legislative proposal led to a debate on the question of how the structure of a union affects the participation of the individual worker, then to an exchange over the proper function of the labor movement in a pluralistic society, and finally to the most basic issues of the survival of freedom in a world becoming totally industrialized. This complexity of points of view and their relation to larger problems makes any summary inevitably oversimplified. However, certain basic themes and the various attitudes toward them can be identified.

There were discussions which centered specifically on legislative proposals and raised such questions as these: What is the extent of corruption and antidemocracy in the labor movement today? Should the trade union be treated more as a voluntary association, or as a "quasi-public" institution reflecting the recognition it has received in law? Would a "reserved powers" approach to legislation generate a tendency within the unions themselves toward reform? Should the labor movement promulgate a bill of rights for the protection of the rights of individuals and groups within unions?

Debate on these specific problems quickly led the conference to broader questions: Is the structure of a trade union conducive to membership participation? Are the values of political democracy analogous to those we seek in the labor movement, or does the difference in function between these two institutions require a basic amendment of this comparison? Should the unions extend their social and political role in order to become more democratic, or is such an approach contrary to the larger, democratic, pluralistic values of the society as a whole?

The conference also considered these issues as they related to the fate of the society as a whole: Should the unions struggle against the alienation which allegedly pervades our complex industrial life? Can they become the instrument of achieving a sweeping transformation of social existence?

Law and Unions.—The discussion of proposed legislation centered on Archibald Cox's paper, and continued throughout the meetings. The most persistent themes were the extent of the abuses in the labor movement; the possibility of a "reserved power" approach to labor law; the "public" character of the unions; and the variety of union structures as a factor in making uniform legislation difficult.

The goal of democratic functioning in the labor movement was defined during the conference by Arthur Goldberg. There seemed to be a consensus that these were the values at stake: Democracy in the labor movement means the right of the worker to full and free participation in the self-government of his union; the right to vote periodically for local and national officers; the right to stand for, and to hold, union office on the basis of uniform qualifications; the right to voice views as to the way the union should act; the right to fair treatment in the application of union laws. No particular forms should be imposed to guarantee these rights, Goldberg insisted; in addition, he felt that the rights implied a correlative obligation upon the member to support the union as an institution.

There was considerable difference among the speakers on the extent of trade-union abuse of these rights. In general, those who urged that information on this subject was scanty were opposed to basic labor legislation at this time, and those who felt that the abuses had been sufficiently documented tended to favor the enactment of some laws which would give a public guarantee to unionists that their rights would be respected.

One trade unionist, for example, held that there has been no proof of widespread abuse in union elections and, since this was so, there should not be any legislative proposals to allow government intervention in the labor electoral process. At the same time he indicated two areas where he felt the problem was sufficiently clear to warrant action: one, where the unions control job opportunities; and, two, where there has been union racial discrimination. He felt that the latter issue was not the primary responsibility of the unions (the labor movement, he argued, had the best record on this score of any of our institutions) but of society as a whole. The real solution, he said, was the passage of a fair-employment-practices law. There are abuses, he concluded, which require laws, but they must be defined and documented, and legislation must be confined to the area where it is actually needed. To "sneak in pet schemes" not immediately related to proven necessity, he said, would make it less likely that law will be passed where it is needed.

One participant took issue with the assertion that the labor movement was making great strides in eliminating discrimination. Formalities, he said, are not determinant, and the fact that various internationals do not have lily-white clauses does not mean that the problem is being solved. He pointed to two specific cases—a carpenters' local in Terre Haute and an IBEW shop in Cleveland—where racial discrimination was practiced despite official statements. He argued that legislative action appears to be a desirable means of dealing with this problem.

Another disputed question dealt with the record of the AFL-CIO in reforming itself, and the prospects for further action along this line. One view, fairly typical of the attitude of trade unionists present, and put forward by one of their number, held that the development of the Ethical Practices Code was the culmination of a long and voluntary process considerably pre-dating the investigations of the McClellan Congressional Committee. As examples he cited the expulsion of the Communist-dominated unions by the CIO, the action against the ILA taken by the AFL, and the merger provisions on corruption adopted by the AFL-CIO. Others were dissatisfied with this analysis. They felt that the data did not indicate a strong tendency toward self-reform on the part of the unions, some arguing, for example, that the CIO's solution of the Communist problem was a belated one.

There was no consensus, then, in defining the extent of antidemocratic and corrupt practices in the labor movement. Some felt that the magnitude of the problem had not been well-documented, that the labor movement was dealing with the situation in its own way in important areas; others were convinced that the evidence was clear and that it indicated a fairly widespread tendency toward abuse in a significant minority of the unions. Everyone agreed on the necessity to organize a careful investigation into the question, but the first group urged that the study precede any legislation and the second held that it should be simultaneous with new laws.

Private, Public or Quasi-Public?—Is the trade union a private, quasi-public, or public institution? Those who emphasized the voluntary-association character of the unions tended to be hostile to most of the current legislative proposals (and to state intervention in general); those who stressed the legal and official status of the unions usually advocated Congressional reform.

A lawyer emphasized the public aspect of the labor movement and found considerable support for this point of view among the conferees. The unions, he said, receive a delegation of power through law, since it is public policy to favor collective bargaining. Given this fact, it is logical that society require conformity to public policy in the area of union democracy, and this well might be enforced through the courts. This last point—judicial rather than legislative intervention—elicited excited comment, and most of those who agreed on the quasi-public character of the labor movement cited this attitude as an argument in favor of legislative reform.

The opposite point of view was also stated. Labor's rights, one conferee emphasized, are not a gift of government but the product of a long struggle on the part of the unions. The fact that this country was relatively late in giving official sanction to this process should not make us think, he said, that there is a basis for arguing that the "legal" place of the labor movement is a point in favor of legislative reform.

This position—and the related debate over the strength and stability of the unions—was persistent throughout the meetings. One conferee, commenting upon the paper delivered by David Cole, felt that any reference to public policy (in Cole's case, in favor of stable units for collective bargaining) necessarily implied a correlative obligation by the unions to give adequate representation to the web of conflicting interests which they contained. And, in another context, a participant took sharp issue with Sumner Slichter's assertion that there was "minute" regulation of collective bargaining by the government.

The debate over the character of trade-union association led almost immediately to a larger question: the desirability of seeking to draw an analogy between the political life of society as a whole and the internal life of the trade unions. Those who attacked this analogy and emphasized the differences between political and trade-union democracy also tended to be hostile to proposals for legislation at this time. As one speaker said, democracy is elusive and cannot be guaranteed by a "gadget approach" toward the labor movement.

Thus, the unresolved lines of argument on the "public" status of the unions fell into two general patterns: those who emphasized the privileges granted by law to the labor movement and who therefore sought to make this recognition a basis for arguing in favor of state (judicial or legislative) intervention; and those who emphasized the voluntary character of the unions and were consequently opposed to any widespread government action in this area. As with most of the debates at the conference, the differences in factual definition were not sharp on this point, but this did not minimize the opposition in the conclusions drawn.

Reserved Powers.—One suggestion, discussed throughout the conference, received support from almost all points of view. This was the conception of a "reserved powers" approach. The speaker who raised this point initially saw considerable abuses in the labor movement. But, he continued, there were many inadequacies in thinking that the law would be a real answer to the problem. Therefore, he urged that the law state a public policy on the democratic rights that should be enjoyed by trade unionists, providing for intervention only if the National Labor Relations Board or the secretary of labor determined that the unions were failing to live up to the general requirements stated by the Congress. In this way, a maximum impulse would be given toward union self-reform and a way would have been found to allay the fears of state interference on the part of sincere and democratic unionists and unions.

Another speaker gave his views of how this general approach might be made specific: An exemption from government intervention, limited to two years, might be granted by the secretary of labor to a union which complied with public policy. If a public review board, such as now exists in the UAW, were part of the exemption, the secretary could prepare a panel and the unions would have to draw upon this group to staff their boards.

A trade unionist argued in favor of a *prima facie* exemption for all unions in the AFL-CIO on the basis of their adherence to the Ethical Practices Code. He laid particular stress on a law requiring full disclosure as a means of implementing a "reserved powers" approach and as a valuable technique for reform in general.

One other suggestion on how to spell out the "reserved powers" approach was offered: Congress should establish a blue-ribbon commission with the initial task of establishing standards of public policy in matters of trade-union democracy. The commission would then formulate a series of rules and submit these to the labor movement. Six months would be given to the unions to bring themselves into conformity with the recommendations. At the end of that time, the situation would be surveyed and the commission would propose a detailed law to the Congress.

Although the discussion on the "reserved powers" approach was not thorough enough to establish a consensus on any particular way of implementing it, the proposal itself appeared to win wide support among the conferees. There was some dissent; two speakers felt that this kind of law might well put Congress in a position where it could dictate principles to the labor movement and then require conformity, and this, they felt, might lead to a dangerous measure of government interference in the internal affairs of the labor movement. However, on the whole, a willingness to consider the idea of "reserved powers" was probably the major consensus achieved at the conference.

The Stability of Unions.—In general, those conferees who stressed the strength of management, the weakness of various unions, and the problems of recession were opposed to anything that would hamper the striking power of organized workers—and they usually included in this any sweeping legislative program providing for government intervention in the labor movement. On the other hand, those who believed that the unions had achieved a considerable and stable place in the society were more willing to think in terms of new laws guaranteeing the rights of the worker against arbitrary and antidemocratic exercise of power on the part of the unions themselves.

The major discussion of this question took place following the summary of Sumner Slichter's paper, which took the position that American trade unionism had become sufficiently strong to require a legislative counterpressure. But the issue had arisen earlier when a sociologist stated that the unions were not in any danger of destruction but on the contrary were strong enough to constitute a threat to the freedom of individual workers and to minority oppositions within the unions. The handling of their recent opposition slates by the Mineworkers, the Teamsters, the Carpenters, and the Steelworkers were cited. Furthermore, the speaker said, the argument that the unions should be immune from external reform is like the corporation plea in the 'thirties to the same effect, and it is as wrong.

This position evoked a sharp retort. One speaker held that the past fifteen years has been a period of management domination, and that the unions had to fear the desire by at least a section of American business to destroy collective bargaining. He argued that Mr. Slichter's assignment of considerable economic power to the unions was a serious error. In reality, he said, management has found it expedient to share some of its increasing profits with the unions and to pass the cost on to other, unorganized groups in the society, but this merely justifies the statement that the unions have a residual influence on wages. Today, with unemployment, new areas of danger to the unions are opening up.

There was also a middle group on this subject. One conferee distinguished between the stable and powerful unions such as the Auto and Steel Workers and those in depressed industries or in a less advantageous economic and organizational position. Another told of the existence of weak situations within strong unions, citing a Steelworker local in West Virginia with 300 union members, which was defeated in a strike by the importation of strikebreakers. A third speaker challenged what he considered the implicit assumption of the argument—that the unions can afford democracy in periods of stability and quiet but abandon it at a time of external challenge. In reality, he argued, the truth is the opposite. In periods of outside pressure, unions must call upon the membership for conscious and voluntary support; in unions unchallenged from without the tendency is toward dictatorial developments. Thus, one of the sharpest divisions of the conference came in the attempt to define the relative strength and weight of the unions in American society.

There was more agreement on a limited area of union strength: where there is job control. One of the conferees who rejected most of the legislation now proposed as irrelevant, nevertheless felt that the facts of the situation warranted legislative concern. Another pointed out that a special difficulty arose when access to a trade is controlled through an apprentice system. Still another stressed that job-rationing by a union was often a necessity in certain trades if a fair order of priority and seniority was to be achieved. No specific proposals came out of this exchange (although one speaker cited the Massachusetts law which forbids exclusion from the union, except on certain *bona fide* grounds, where there is job control), but it was agreed that the situation required particular consideration and could not be included in the generalizations applying to certain mass-production industries.

The Unions' Lack of Uniformity.—A lawyer questioned the assumption that there is sufficient uniformity in the labor movement to permit the development of a single program covering all conditions. He felt that the labor movement is in constant revolution, so much so that it cannot even be assumed that democracy is a proper antidote to corruption. A trusteeship, he said, can be used to aid the fight against corruption, but it can also be an instrument of antidemocratic arbitrariness. Another speaker, reënforcing this point, cited the vested interest of a local union leadership as one of the problems beyond the range of legislative resolution.

On the other side, one conferee felt that the picture of great complexity was spurious and that there is a certain community, a set of uniform features, in the labor movement which should make it possible to pass adequate legislation. A lawyer argued that the unions could themselves promulgate a bill of rights, such as the American Civil Liberties Union has proposed, or adopt procedures which have been advocated by organizations like the Workers Defense League, if only because, in some cases, state action, even under the best conditions, is too ponderous and too long in achieving justice.

Labor and Law: An Over-all View.—There was no consensus on the question of labor and the law. Almost everyone was ready to agree on a general conception of what democracy should mean in the unions. Many could favor the over-all idea of a "reserved powers" approach to the problem. But there were fairly sharp, and unresolved, disputes on factual questions, such as the extent of antidemocratic and corrupt practices in the labor movement, the stability of unions, the threat from without, and so on. These differences determined attitudes on the unions' ability for self-reform, the applicability of a uniform legislative approach to a complex situation, the economic influence of the unions, and their responsibility for inflation.

Roughly, there were two polar attitudes: the one based on a feeling that extensive abuses in the labor movement have not been documented, that the unions are still threatened, that most of the present legislative proposals are "gimmicky"; the other based on the view that proof of extensive corruption is now available, that the unions have achieved a secure status in our society, and that external pressure is necessary to guarantee individual and minority rights against a new bureaucracy. In general, the conferees who were active in the labor movement itself tended toward the first view, though with exceptions, and were opposed to suggestions that legislation was needed at the present time. Some of the labor scholars, lawyers, and others agreed with this. But the bulk of those who favored new laws were not professionally active in the union movement.

Worker Participation and New Functions.—Discussion about proposed legislation continued throughout the conference, as did discussion of the broader question of worker participation in unions—democracy considered substantively as a social process and not just objectively as a legal right.

At the outset a speaker argued that the real problem was to achieve a vigorous internal life in the unions. The fact that there are no observable abuses, he said, does not demonstrate that there is democracy. Even when the legal rights of workers and minorities are guaranteed, there is no assurance that a full and free discussion will follow within the union. Consequently, he concluded, an aim of legislation should be that of "vitalizing factional life" within the unions. Although it may be that law alone cannot achieve this, it may still be an impetus toward it.

Another participant reënforced this point, suggesting that the country might try to build "inducements" into its labor law which would set a premium on active participation. One possible method, he noted, would be to require a member who seeks to make use of the union appellate procedure to demonstrate that he has actually availed himself of the other opportunities provided for his participation in the decision-making process, such as attendance at meetings, voting in elections, and the like.

These views were challenged by a conferee who held that participation in union affairs cannot be equated with attendance at union meetings. Indeed, he thought, there is some contradiction in electing responsible officers and then reviewing all decisions at a "town meeting" of the local. He suggested that the labor movement might consider a representative system at the local level itself; later in the conference the efforts of the Newspaper Guild to develop such a system of local representative assemblies were described.

Another school of thought argued against the analogy between political and trade-union society as it related to the question of worker participation. One speaker described a situation in which the union adhered to all the democratic rules during a factional struggle and suffered destructive consequences because of it. Another felt that a dedicated and professionalized leadership was more decisive in achieving union democracy than rank-and-file movements.

These considerations led, in turn, to a discussion of the function of the union in the society. One participant argued that it was impossible to think of membership participation when all it meant was voting for officers every three years. To achieve real participation, he continued, it was necessary to expand the activities of the union itself. Only through a "multi-function" union, he felt, could one achieve a high level of participation. On the other hand, it was also said that the multi-function union could be a vehicle for bureaucratic paternalism. The *kind* of expanded functions, this speaker continued, was crucial to the problem of getting more membership participation in union affairs.

In general, it was agreed that democracy in the unions must be made substantive, that there must be active participation of the membership in the decision-making process. But the *means* of achieving this goal were various—legal "inducement," the restructuring of the union meeting, the expansion of union functions. Along with the agreement on the desirability of a high degree of participation there arose some basic differences about the structure of the trade union in relation to a democratic internal life.

One speaker said that the "special problem" of democracy in the labor movement was control over power and, more particularly, the ability to remove a power-wielding person from office. The way in which the worker participates in the union is different from his role in political society; indeed, the conditions of trade-union existence do not provide a sustained basis for continuing participation. Therefore, he asked, if the life of the unions is not conducive to membership participation, how can the goal of limiting power be achieved? Several answers were suggested: first, through the activity of outside groups (such as the Workers Defense League), which attempt to vitalize the trade-union system; secondly, through the influence of tradition, a factor which is apparently of some force in England but not so important in the United States; and, thirdly, through law—through external reform, which guarantees to the society as a whole that the limitation of power in the labor movement will be effectively carried out.

Another speaker developed a similar analysis. We must be concerned, he said, with the "structural prerequisites for democracy" in the unions. As an example, he cited the situation in the Miners' Union. In the old days, the locals used to carry on negotiations as to rates at the pit. This function provided for participation on the part of the miners who were immediately affected. Today, however, this function is centralized—and impetus toward democratic participation has been lost. In fact, this conferee continued, the growth of paternalism in the labor movement may be seen as the psychological concomitant of a more bureaucratized system of collective bargaining.

This point of view led to a lively debate. One speaker, who more or less summarized a trend of thought opposed to that of the two conferees just quoted, felt that some of the talk about participation constituted a refusal to accept the union on its own terms. The labor movement, he declared, is an "imperfect going concern" and must not be viewed primarily as a mechanism for individual self-realization; we should not project our own images onto the unions; we should not conceive of them as an exercise in democracy, but rather as functional institutions which have aspects of democracy.

On this point, the conflict did not seem to be one of formal definition—almost everyone agreed that membership participation was a desirable goal—but of emphasis. For some, the collective economic function of the union (the "imperfect going concern") was the major factor. To others, the quality of life within the local was at least as important, though related to the other function. This disagreement was not resolved.

The proper function of the labor movement—one of the most persistent themes at the conference—received specific attention after Slichter's statement that unions must develop a larger social concern. One speaker pointed out that the unions were facing a new era, and it was imperative for them to incorporate a larger social purpose into the movement. He said the coming period would be characterized by considerable unemployment, chronic distress in durable consumer goods, and serious structural difficulties in industries. Another conferee also stressed economic factors in his advocacy of increased political action. There is a limit, he argued, to the ability of the unions to change the economy by collective bargaining—a limit that becomes even more obvious in a time of administered prices (in the steel industry, for example, where pay raises were rendered nugatory by price increases). Consequently, the issue of price control, which can be effected only through political trade-union action, is likely to become of even more importance in the future. He did not advocate the formation of a labor party but, rather, the extension of union action within the present framework.

The assumption of these speakers that the labor movement has lost its momentum in the areas of social policy was questioned. One person cited recent successes in labor's fight to improve the social-security laws; he also discounted some of the claims that employer support for federal social-security plans has grown because the plans represent a substitute for those negotiated by unions.

The discussion of the broader social role of the unions received added impetus in the exchange occasioned by Erich Fromm's paper. One speaker took issue with the consensus that seemed to have developed in favor of expanding the functions of the unions. The central issue, he said, is that of pluralism. If this is a crucial democratic value, do we want the unions to enter into political action on a wide scale and thereby reduce the number and spread of the centers of social and political action? He cited the trade unions in Belgium, where the Christian and Socialist trade unionists hardly speak to each other, as a demonstration of the harmful effect of multifunctional unionism. Thus, he felt that the expansion of union functions would defeat pluralism in the society as a whole. Another participant spoke in defense of "limited unionism." Union members, he said, are active in many other areas of the society, and this is good. There was a real danger, he felt, in building up a relatively monolithic trade-union apparatus and thus destroying important centers of freedom and individual action. A partisan of broader social action on the part of the unions accepted both of these criticisms. A monolithic approach was indeed dangerous, he said, and the Belgian example was one we should carefully avoid imitating. But within the context of pluralism, he continued, the union movement must be a socially advanced element and it is a loss that, unlike in the 'thirties, those who are for progressive social changes no longer look to the unions for democratic action.

To sum up, there was consensus in the value of making democracy in the unions "substantive," that is, making it a matter of membership participation in decision-making. But there was considerable difference on the relative importance of decision-making. On the question of whether a new social vision and function is necessary to the continuing development of the labor movement as a whole, the exchange moved between the polarities of "social purpose" and "limited function" unionism, with each side tending to grant the validity of the opposition's criticism.

Some Cases.—On three occasions during the conference, the discussion centered on specific cases: the experience of the English labor movement, the experience of the Australian labor movement, and the functioning of the review boards set up by the Auto Workers and the Upholsterers' Unions.

J. R. McClelland's talk focused upon the fact that the Australian labor movement accepted, and even advocated, government intervention, not only into the collective-bargaining process but into the internal life of the unions as well. The questions after his paper revolved around two points: the workability of this system, particularly as it affects wages and hours; and the reasons for the striking differences in attitude between Australian and American unions.

McClelland was asked if the Australian unions had made any great gains in winning wages and hours, welfare funds, and the like. He replied that the Australian workers had achieved a forty-hour week and a relatively high standard of wages, but that they lagged behind in the development of pension funds. He did cite, however, the "long-service leave" —a three-month paid vacation at the end of twenty years of service—as a significant "fringe" benefit.

McClelland, who had described the influence which the Communist party had achieved in the labor movement, was asked how this had happened. His reasons included the apathy of the rank and file, the crookedness of some election manipulations, the Communist ability to leave politics out of the union fight, and the fact that some Labor party left-wingers were willing to bloc with the Communists in a united "left" front. This led to questions concerning the rights of expelled workers in Australia. McClelland said that exclusion from the union meant, in fact, if not in law, exclusion from the industry.

Do the Australian unions manage to achieve a high degree of membership participation? McClelland replied that there was much apathy, but he did not believe that attendance at local meetings should be taken as the decisive criterion. There was a considerable amount of union activity in the shop itself, and this was at least as important as going to a meeting after work was over. He also stated that the legislative approach which Australian labor has accepted has not resulted in any particular increase in membership participation but that the workers do turn out to vote for the Labor party, with some 60 to 70 per cent voting in elections.

On the question of the difference between the attitudes of American and Australian labor toward the state, McClelland declared that the fifty-year existence of a Labor party as the political arm of the workers was the decisive factor in orienting them toward state action. One of the participants, however, felt that the reasons for difference between the two countries were more numerous—namely, the heterogeneous character of the American work force, and the consequent absence of class consciousness in the Australian sense; the absence of the farmers as a political force in Australia; and the federated structure of government in America which militated against the emergence of a strong Labor party.

After the discussion of the Australian situation with its emphasis on state intervention in the collective-bargaining process and into union life, the conference was told of an opposite development, that of England, where governmental regulation is conspicuously lacking. One of the conferees suggested that the strength of the executive committee in the English unions was a reason for this. The English unions have an elected appeals committee, a system of federated bargaining, and other structural elements which tend to reduce the power of the president. This speaker also stressed traditional factors, such as the custom of open debate and a high sense of official responsibility to the membership.

Another comment, made by a unionist who had studied in England, focused on the cultural differences between England and America as important in determining the mode of operation of the labor movement in each country. However, he also insisted that the unions of the two countries were similar in that they had not achieved a significant participation of the membership in the decision-making process. As one of the reasons for this he referred to the antiquated structure of the British trade unions.

An exchange then developed over the question of the relative strength of British union leadership. One labor historian felt that the Bevin tradition of strong personal leadership was important and contradicted any theory about the weakness of the English union president. He also argued that there was no necessary relation between democracy and the absence of corruption; indeed, he said, it may well be that in certain situations a democratic union may be the means of corruption's winning a victory. A trade unionist agreed with the point on the Bevin tradition in England. He remarked that some unions had lifetime officers, a strong centralization of power, and definite limitations upon the rights of the local branch. Hugh Clegg agreed that the Bevin tradition, so-called, applied to the British steel workers but maintained that his initial description was valid for trade unionism as a whole in his country.

One conferee asked Clegg if the widespread phenomenon of wildcat strikes in England was primarily a result of the stable wage policy which developed under the postwar Labor government. Clegg replied that the tradition had deeper roots. The national leadership of the British unions, he noted, tend to be more "responsible" than locals and the rank and file. This comes out most clearly in a period of wage restraint supported by the leadership (such as took place between 1948 and 1950), but it has a long history. When local opposition does take place, then the shop-steward movement and the strikes associated with it assume a greater importance in union life.

Finally, there was a discussion of the paradox that both England and Australia have Labor parties but have different attitudes on state intervention. Clegg explained that the British

Labour party was preceded by a long history of trade unionism, but in Australia the economic and political wings of the
movement developed together. Furthermore, the Australian
Labor party has been a major influence in Australian politics
for a long time, whereas the British Labour party took over
the government for the first time in 1945.

The discussion of the Australian and British experiences
brought out the importance of cultural and historical factors
in the development of the labor movement in the two countries. The discussion also demonstrated the deep hostility of
American trade unionists toward government intervention in
their affairs.

The last specific case to receive some extended discussion
was that of the public review board. Several points were central to this topic: how wide the jurisdiction of the board should
be; the extent to which the repression of political minority
rights in the unions makes such boards necessary; the possibility of adopting this technique as a basic instrument for dealing
with the problem of corruption and antidemocratic practices.

One participant, who has been associated with a public
review board, felt that the jurisdictional question was still to
be defined. The UAW, he pointed out, has tended to conceive
of the board as having the function of initiating investigations.
This, he felt, was probably not a good thing, for the board
might not be able to carry such a burden. Another conferee
noted that the UAW board had already taken the position that
it would only act in an "adversary" matter—that it would not
come in to pass judgment on a union action unless there were
a claim of injustice. Several speakers felt that this was a good
approach, and that there was a danger of a board's becoming
an agency to "whitewash" the actions of the union administration.

On the problem of political repression of minorities in the
labor movement, one speaker noted that a study of appeals
which come to executive boards shows that most appeals are

nonpolitical and refer to fines levied against workers for violating some provision of the contract or union rules. On the other hand, another speaker felt that it was important to have the review board apparatus available to the members in any event, should some injustice emerge. He argued that the very existence of a board might allow more workers to file claims, and so we cannot now estimate the amount of work required.

One trade unionist said that it might be possible to establish a review board for the entire AFL-CIO, composed of responsible national leaders of the various unions. This proposal met criticism from several quarters, a typical objection being that the national leaders were interested parties, and that the most important thing about the review boards was the guarantee of their complete independence from the pressures of the union administration.

There was one *caveat* expressed by a conferee: the review board, he said, will not remedy all ills. He expressed misgivings about granting an exemption under law to unions simply because they had a review board. This, he felt, might allow the unions to bargain away the rights of the members too cheaply. But the majority of those who spoke felt that the review board system could be established and that competent and truly independent people could be obtained to staff the various boards, even though almost everyone conceded that the problem of obtaining the right personnel would be a serious one, particularly if the review board method were to become general.

Labor and Alienation.—Erich Fromm's talk and the discussion which followed it raised fundamental questions; for Fromm's presentation concentrated attention on the society itself and on the nature of work under contemporary conditions and its effect on the human personality.

One of the first discussants asked: Can a modern factory be humanized? Can all kinds of work be made interesting? Fromm replied that some jobs would remain intrinsically

monotonous no matter what the character of the society, but
still there were possibilities of easing the problem if the work
situation were treated as primarily social and if the technique
of job shifting when the work was basically repetitive were
adopted.

Two participants felt that the issue had to be made more
precise: What can the union do in terms of specific action?
Several answers were proposed. One argued in favor of developing a higher consciousness among the union leadership itself
of the need to transcend the alienation of work. Another discussed the "creative engineering" approach being developed
at MIT and felt that the unions should make the humanization
of machine work an item of negotiation and major interest. In
general, all of these participants accepted the fundamental
premise of Fromm's paper—that the alienation of the worker,
the destruction of human and social relations through the
productive process, was a basic issue in American society today. As one participant put it, the issue is not so much that of
guaranteeing the right to vote to the union member, but,
more basically, a question of providing the worker with real
alternatives for his participation in decision-making.

This theme was related to the recurring call for a "new
faith," a broader purpose within the labor movement. There
were disagreements on the precise nature of this problem. One
conferee, for example, emphasized the danger of union "paternalism" if the labor movement seeks to attack the basic issues.
Pension plans, he pointed out, had resulted in a considerable
restriction on worker mobility, with the Bureau of Labor Statistics' "quit-rate" figures having dropped by half in the course
of a decade. Another participant emphasized the possibilities
of minority domination which are potential in the attempt to
make the union a more thoroughly democratic structure. He
cited a study of a local of the International Ladies' Garment
Workers Union, where it was found that the "normal," adjusted
workers were not the ones who availed themselves of the op-

portunities for democratic participation but rather those workers who had nothing to do with their time. There was considerable dissent from this opinion throughout the discussion of alienation.

In another dissent with Fromm, one participant asked: Was all this talk about the alienated worker a "Ruskinesque myth"? This person felt that the trade unions had indeed been consulted on the question of human engineering and that the deadening and antihuman character of work in the shop had been exaggerated. From this he concluded that the proposals for a new infusion of consciousness into the labor movement precipitated the great danger that the union would end up determining the whole life of the worker. Another conferee, echoing this point of view, stressed the social impact of automation, through which, he argued, we are achieving the goal of freeing the worker from drudgery and of humanizing the work. This thought was summarized by a trade unionist who expressed the belief that the old notion of the worker's being an adjunct to the machine no longer applies and that we may now properly speak of the worker as a "free man."

The opposition between those who stressed the continuing and problematic aspect of worker alienation, and those who emphasized the changes which have taken place over the years, was the most basic one which emerged from the discussion of Fromm's paper.

One discussant agreed that workers lead better lives than they did fifty years ago and that great strides had been made to change the deadening and antihuman life of the factory. But, he continued, there remain "a million jobs" which are destructive of the personalities of those who work them. And the shared hatred of the job is still one of the few real points of community and solidarity among the workers in America's factories, he said. Another conferee said that the evidence demonstrating the widespread existence of alienation is not mythic; this means that the union must go beyond the issue of wages and hours, and deal with some of these questions. The union should negotiate the right of the worker to make choices within the shop and to use his leisure on the line to produce for himself; it should attack outmoded class distinctions, such as those that differentiate the dining rooms for the production workers, the foremen, and the white-collar staff.

On the other side, a conferee asked if alienation were not intrinsic to man throughout history and thus not a specific problem of our industrial society. Fromm agreed that alienation has always been with us and so has the struggle to overcome it. The contradiction between human needs and inhuman processes has been a dynamic and creative force throughout time, he declared. Now we must recapture the vision of humanity ourselves, for when societies no longer respond to a humanistic vision, it is a sign that they are dying. We must now ask: Is this happening to us? We have solved many of the problems of the nineteenth century, Fromm concluded, but we are still confronted by the basic issue of the twentieth century: false collectivism. In responding to it, we must become aware of our concept of man, of our most basic social faith.

Conclusion.—In summary, the Arden House Conference discussion revealed considerable agreement with regard to the areas of concern but a wide range of difference on how to approach the basic problems. The major themes of the conference were proposals for new legislation; the question of vitalizing the internal workings of the unions; and the proper relationship between organized labor and society as a whole. Each of these strands concentrated on a different level of analysis and debate—the immediate and political, the more long-range consideration of the quality of union life, and the ultimate social decision of new directions for the entire society —and yet the discussion was almost never limited to a single perspective but rather related all three approaches.

In the area of proposed legislation, there was sharp difference. The polar positions were those advocating considerable government intervention in union internal life and those opposing any such approach. These specific attitudes were related in turn to different views of the place of the labor movement in contemporary American society. Those who advocated wide-scale intervention tended to see the unions as established, powerful, and basically secure, while the other grouping usually emphasized the elements of precariousness which are still a part of the American labor movement. Both groups, however, agreed that more research was necessary to establish the extent of corruption and undemocratic practices within the unions.

The conference was unanimous on the fact that worker participation in the life of the union is a central problem. Yet there were two counterposed views of approaching this situation. One was to develop a new union faith—a concern for social and political issues which would make labor organization multifunctional. The other view feared that such an undertaking would endanger the pluralism of American society. As a result, the partisans of this conception advocated that techniques for stimulating worker participation should be sought within the framework of "limited function" unionism. Finally, there were those who argued that the very nature of the work situation in our society made the development of rank-and-file democracy in the unions unlikely. They therefore called for government intervention to maintain rights which might be abrogated, not so much through bureaucratic design, but as a result of continued neglect by the members.

Finally, the discussion occasioned by Fromm's paper posed the problem of the dehumanizing tendencies of industrialized society as a whole and the responsibility of the labor movement to act against them. There was disagreement over the accuracy of Fromm's description itself, with some feeling that the alienation which he discussed was disappearing through the development of modern technology itself.

Thus, there was considerable difference on each of the basic themes of the conference. And yet, there was a common feeling that the American labor movement is entering a new phase of its existence, that it will encounter problems which it has never faced before, and that there is a real need for creative thinking if the challenge is to be met.